THE LUDDITES

LIBRARY OF TEXTILE HISTORY

THE LUDDITES

MACHINE-BREAKING IN REGENCY ENGLAND

Malcolm I. Thomis
Senior Lecturer in History, University of Stirling

DAVID & CHARLES
ARCHON BOOKS

The help of the Pasold Research Fund Limited in assisting the publication of this volume is gratefully acknowledged

ISBN 0 7153 4974 0 (*Great Britain*)
ISBN 0 208 01447 1 (*United States*)

COPYRIGHT NOTICE

This edition first published in 1970 in Great Britain by David & Charles (Publishers) Limited, Newton Abbot, Devon, and in the United States by Archon Books, Hamden, Connecticut

Set in eleven point Times New Roman two points leaded
and printed in Great Britain
by Bristol Typesetting Company Limited

CONTENTS

To the late J. D. Chambers
who first introduced me to the Luddites

ILLUSTRATIONS

Chapter One

MACHINE-BREAKERS
AND LUDDITES

THE LUDDITES PRESENT initially a problem of definition. It is useless to write or argue about them unless their identity is clear.

Employers were being threatened by letters signed 'Ned Ludd' in December 1811, and in that month the *Nottingham Review* carried reports of stocking-frame breakers or 'Luddites as they are now called'. The name was first used, it seems, of men who broke stocking-frames in 1811, and shortly afterwards John Blackner, a historian of Nottingham, proffered an explanation of the term which has satisfied most historians since that day. Blackner suggested that 'the framebreakers assumed this appellation from the circumstance of an ignorant youth, in Leicestershire, of the name of Ludlam, who, when ordered by his father, a framework-knitter, to square his needles, took a hammer and beat them into a heap'; when frame-breaking began in Nottingham in 1811 Ludlam was remembered and his name was adopted by the frame-breakers. As machine-breaking spread in 1812 from the hosiery and lace trades of the east Midlands into first the woollen industry of the West Riding of Yorkshire and then the cotton industry of south Lancashire and north Cheshire, it was natural that the same term should be applied to machine-breaking in these different contexts. And as contemporaries were ready to use it to cover the different kinds of machine-breaking in the years 1811-16, so have some historians accepted it as the generic term for machine-breakers whatever their time and place in history. Thus a recent examination of the breaking of thresh-ing-machines in southern England in 1830 has talked of 'agricultural Luddism' and concluded that 'Lud's true name was Swing', for the fabulous Captain Swing was the most suc-cessful machine-breaker of them all and way ahead of the fabu-lous General Ludd in his achievements. And if the historian has taken over the term for all of history's machine-breakers, so has the layman accepted it for all those who resist mechani-sation, automation and the like, and who are the supposed enemies of 'progress' where the adoption of labour-saving devices is concerned.[1]

Machine-breaking was, of course, by no means a new phen-omenon when it appeared in Nottinghamshire in March 1811, being almost a time-honoured tradition among certain occu-pational groups. Early attacks on machinery were recorded in Restoration times and continued to be recorded into Victorian times. In a period of increasingly widespread legislation against trade-union activity, which culminated in the comprehensive codification of 1799-1800, orthodox negotiation between em-ployers and representatives of the men, supplemented where necessary by a withdrawal of labour, was not a viable proposi-tion. Industrial workers tended, anyhow, not to be concen-trated in towns in a way which made their organisation for trade-union purposes possible, but to be scattered throughout the countryside with minimal contacts with each other. In these circumstances the sophisticated techniques of a modern trade union, supported by the ultimate sanction of a properly organised strike, were impossible. Instead, there was machine-breaking, or 'collective bargaining by riot', which could effectively and quickly strike at an offensive local employer.[2]

Machine-breaking, or the threat of it, was, it has been sug-gested, the basis of power of a number of early trade unions; besides constituting a threat to be held out against employers, it was also a means of combating blacklegs and ensuring solidarity in industrial disputes. In the campaigns of the Spitalfields weavers, for instance, in the late 1760s, assaults on looms served a double purpose of hitting out at wage-cutting employers and bringing into line those workmen who were not co-operating with the rest by contributing to strike funds.[3]

Machine-breaking in the eighteenth century, it has been said, was used primarily for bringing pressure to bear upon employers for one purpose or another. In 1710 a London hosier who had infringed Charles II's Charter to the Worshipful Company of Framework-Knitters by taking no fewer than forty-nine apprentices at one time, had his frames broken in consequence. In 1779, following their abortive attempt to secure parliamentary regulation for the hosiery trade, the framework-knitters of Nottingham in their anger broke the frames of their employers in what the Hammonds have described as 'characteristic fashion'. Ten years later the *Nottingham Journal* reported another incident when men with blackened faces smashed a frame of unacceptable width. All the grievances against which the framework-knitters protested, excessive employment of apprentices, absence of parliamentary regulation, and the use of wide frames, were present in the Luddite period in Nottinghamshire, and it is correct to place Midlands Luddism within this context of collective bargaining by riot and the pressurising of employers by the use of force. Early examples of these can also be found inside another industry, the woollen cloth trade, which was again to feature prominently in the Luddism of 1812. The West of England clothworkers, for instance, repeatedly pressed their demands upon their employers at various times in the eighteenth century by attacking both their industrial and private property. And similar behaviour has been recorded amongst the coal-miners; riots in Northumberland in the 1740s involved the breaking of pit-head machinery and won wage increases, while an outburst of machine-breaking in 1765 won for the men the right to select new employers when their annual contracts had expired. The Luddite period of 1811-16 saw traditional practices being pursued as the machine breakers of the Midlands used the vulnerability of their em-

ployers' property as a means of attempting to bring pressure
to bear upon them over their various demands.[4]

These attacks on machines did not imply any necessary
hostility to machinery as such; machinery was just a con-
veniently exposed target against which an attack could be
made. Just as the Luddism of 1811-16 was to consist of a
mixture of coercion of employers by violence and anti-
machinery demonstrations, so were both these elements present
in the century and a half that preceded 1811. Hostility to
labour-saving machinery was no new feature of English life,
as a whole code of medieval and early modern paternalist,
protective legislation clearly indicates, and attacks upon such
machinery were a well-established feature of the industrial
scene well before the time of the Luddites. But examples have
been cited of the unopposed introduction of machinery into
the mining and printing industries where improvements did
not threaten the position of existing groups of workers. A
particularly noteworthy example of this, since it concerns
areas and industries so much implicated in machine-breaking
on other occasions, was the warm welcome given to the
pioneers of cotton-spinning, Hargreaves and Arkwright, in
Nottingham in the second half of the eighteenth century, after
they had been allegedly driven from Lancashire by working-
class hostility to their inventions. In their own areas their work
appeared to threaten the livelihood of established interests;
in Nottingham it would be a valuable supplement to the existing hosiery trade and offer the alternative employment of
cotton-spinning to workmen, whose opportunities were thereby
enlarged.[5]

But such a convenient harmonising of interests did not exist
everywhere, and conflict often followed industrial innovation
and mechanical invention. When Dutch or engine looms were
brought over to London at the beginning of the seventeenth
century there were complaints against the use of 'engines for
workinge of tape, lace, ribbon, and such, wherein one man
doth more amongst them than seven English men can doe',
and in 1638 the Crown, confirming and extending the Charter

of the London weavers, banned the use of these machines. In 1675 the weavers of Spitalfields rioted for three days against machines which could, allegedly, do the work of twenty men. Over a century later the engine-weavers were believed to be the cause of great distress to the narrow-weavers because they could do six times the normal amount of work, and in January 1768 attacks were made by the single-hand weavers against their opponents' looms. Another almost classical case of an anti-machinery attack in London was the assault on a mechanical sawmill by 500 sawyers in 1768.[6]

The cloth-finishers had repeatedly proclaimed their hostility to new machinery before the crisis year of 1812. Tudor legislation of 1551-2 had suppressed gig-mills but had been difficult to enforce, and a century later popular clamour had provoked a strengthened prohibition through a royal proclamation. In 1737 finishers in the Lancashire woollen areas complained that machinery was being extensively used and that cloth was being dressed at one-third the normal cost, causing their hands to lose work. The campaign against the gig-mill and the more recent shearing-frame, which together threatened to render valueless the traditional skill of the cropper in raising the nap of woollen cloth and cutting it level, turned to violent machine-breaking riots in the last years of the eighteenth and early years of the nineteenth century. These were particularly serious in the West Country woollen areas, though it was in the West Riding sector that many years of bitter opposition to machinery, old and new, finally culminated in the Luddite outbreaks of 1812. It is known that a shop containing gig-mills at Holbeck, Leeds, was burnt to the ground by an irate populace 'about thirteen years' before the troubles of 1812, and there were possibly other such cases in Leeds, for the manufacturers of that town were effectively subdued into suspending attempts to introduce the unpopular machinery. A few years later, in 1802, all gig-mills which had been introduced into Huddersfield shops were evidently 'totally stopt from working' by action from the croppers, though this was no more than a passing triumph and no effective deterrent to the experiments of later innovators.[7]

But it was, not surprisingly, the Lancashire cotton industry which experienced most cases of machine-destruction during the eighteenth century. In 1758 a man was arraigned at Lancaster Assizes for threatening to burn down the engine-house of a Manchester merchant, Garside, and it is thought that this case probably arose out of the current weavers' dispute and the opposition to the recent introduction of the swivel-loom for small-ware weaving. In 1768 and 1769 there were riots in and around Blackburn; in the second phase, in February and March 1769, a mob of a hundred attempted to pull down looms at Oswaldtwistle and Blackburn. The precise nature of these riots is in some doubt, but it seems probable that one phase was the spinning-jenny riots which were responsible, according to the story handed down, for driving Hargreaves, the inventor of the jenny, out of Lancashire, though there is some obscurity concerning the dating of the jenny riots and Hargreaves' departure for Nottingham. The most serious outburst, however, occurred in the autumn of 1779, when Arkwright's water-frames and carding-engines were destroyed as well as spinning-jennies, and it is interesting to note the participation of colliers and labourers in this cotton-trade dispute. It is also of some interest to observe that the crowds left the jennies of twenty-four spindles or under untouched, destroying only the bigger machines, with a view, evidently, to attempting to keep spinning by jenny as a domestic industry by eliminating the machines that had to be housed in factories. In the event, the displaced spinners were absorbed readily enough in the fast-expanding weaving side of the industry, and it was to be in connection with weaving that Lancashire became involved in Luddism in 1812. Already, in 1792, there had been a declared opposition to steam-loom weaving and this had been manifested in an attack on Grimshaw's factory at Manchester, which contained twenty-four of Cartwright's patent looms. The factory was burnt down by angry handloom weavers, who anticipated by twenty years the action of the Lancashire Luddites who similarly mobilised against power looms in 1812.[8]

And so it can be seen clearly enough that Luddism, the machine-breaking which started in 1811, was part of a well-established pattern of behaviour amongst industrial workers. The novelty of the events of the years 1811-16 lies rather in their coincidence and in their intensity than in their nature.

This is not an attempt to describe the entire phenomenon of machine-breaking through the ages, or to assess comprehensively the importance of resistance to mechanisation as a factor in industrial growth. It is more modestly an account of those who broke machinery in the years 1811-16, though this does not mean that all ambiguities about the meaning of terms are now at an end. The adaptations and distortions of later generations are as nothing compared with the confusions of contemporaries when they discussed the subject, and it is these confusions which must now be examined.

The distinction drawn by one historian between 'Luddism proper' and 'what was called Luddism' is a distinction which sympathetic observers were concerned to make at the time. The less sympathetic were less inclined to discriminate between the law-breakers who were involved in machine-wrecking and other people who were simultaneously carrying out illegal activities of other kinds or who were simply involved in one of the many protest movements of the time which coincided with Luddism but had not necessarily any close connection with it. The *Leeds Intelligencer* specifically admitted in December 1812 that it recognised no distinction between Luddites and thieves and robbers, by which it presumably meant that all were criminals and all equally bad. Others would undoubtedly have wished to add food rioters, trade unionists, parliamentary reformers, and other radicals to this list of groups who might suitably have been classified, and were in fact classified, with the machine-breakers as Luddites who disturbed the peace and tranquillity of Regency England, acting illegally or simply in a manner unacceptable to the respectable elements of society. The strands of Luddism are then difficult to separate, and it is useful to look at the other forms of

B

unacceptable behaviour that were being practised at this time
and with which Luddism was repeatedly confused. This is
not to prejudge the issue of whether the Luddites were or were
not something more than industrial saboteurs with industrial
aims, or to claim that Luddism was something entirely separate from contemporaneous conflicts. It is simply to state that a
lot of other activities were going on at the same time as Luddism which would have gone on anyhow, with which Luddism
became in the popular mind confused and, as far as many
commentators are concerned, closely connected. There is a
not uncommon view that every act of industrial organisation
from incipient trade unionism to violent sabotage, every act of
political agitation from that of the mild reformer to that of
the blood-seeking revolutionary, and every conceivable crime
from petty larceny to murder, were somehow, in the years
1811-18, the work of the Luddites. An almighty crime wave
swept over England and this was Luddism; at any rate this
is often seen as Luddism.[9]

Part of the problem is to distinguish Luddism from this
general outbreak of crime which seems to have accompanied
and in part derived from it. There is plenty of evidence to
suggest that many of the alleged Luddites were in fact simply
criminals who would have existed at any time but flourished
particularly at this time amidst the general unrest. As early as
5 December 1811 a correspondent from Crich in Derbyshire
made the prediction, to the Home Secretary, that unless Luddism were speedily stopped all sorts of depredations would be
committed under cover of frame-breaking; highway-robbers
and housebreakers were very numerous, he wrote, and a dread-
ful winter lay ahead. This prediction was particularly well
fulfilled in Yorkshire. At the subsequent Yorkshire Assizes in
January 1813 Mr Justice Le Blanc traced the growth of Luddism from an anti-machinery movement, through a campaign
of robbery for the possession of fire-arms, into a series of
thefts by force of property of every description, leaving the
original cause of the movement entirely behind. The Leeds
press reported in September and October 1812 that prisoners

were daily being brought in on charges of robbery under cover of Luddism, and the Lord-Lieutenant of the West Riding, Lord Fitzwilliam, received the comment that machinery had become a mere excuse for private assassination and robbery. By November Fitzwilliam saw plunder as the only real objective of the law-breakers; even the fire-arms, which had interested the robbers at an earlier stage, were now seized only if they happened to come by them in the course of their evening's work. And when Colonel Norton wrote to the Huddersfield magistrate, Joseph Radcliffe, about the seventeen Luddites executed at York, he said that he considered that only eight were real Luddites; nine were depredators who took advantage of the time.[10]

These people believed that Luddism, while separate from conventional crime, was an incitement to it. Others simply made no distinction between Luddism and plain crime. The *Leeds Intelligencer,* for instance, reported in July 1812 that General Ludd had evidently begun his operations in Leeds, and substantiated this by listing the thefts that had recently occurred. Even the *Mercury*, which usually reported Luddism carefully and sympathetically, slipped into the language of its opponents when it reported on 5 December 1812 the resurgence of a violent spirit of Luddism at Huddersfield, which it illustrated by citing several examples of robbery with violence by an organised gang of criminals in the area. One confessing member, James Hay, suggested that the Luddites were organised in parties of ten for their activities, but it is clear from his account that he was simply a robber who stole money and watches, though a robber who called himself a Luddite. And so it is not surprising that a Yorkshire annalist should describe the robberies of the time as his account of Yorkshire Luddism in 1812.[11]

In fact the authorities of the day appraised the situation much more coolly and accurately than this confusion would perhaps suggest. Mr Allison wrote from Huddersfield on 15 September to inform the Home Secretary that Radcliffe had committed Batley, Fisher and Lamb, who seemed to be nothing but a set of desperate housebreakers who had taken advantage of the times to keep the neighbourhood in a state of alarm; Allison feared that there were many nests of thieves still to be broken into as well as some secret organisations amongst the croppers, but he did not confuse the two. Similarly, General Maitland, in charge of operations against the Luddites, reported on 5 November that some organised robbery was still going on in the neighbourhood of Halifax, but that this was something entirely separate from the Luddite combination. It is simply not enough to state that one or two groups of housebreakers who masqueraded as Luddites confused the picture. As far as contemporaries were concerned, the imitators had taken over from the real ones and were just as much a problem as their models. A real crime explosion was detonated by the Luddites and the masqueraders must not be dismissed so lightly because they were debasing the coinage of real Luddism, which was highly motivated and heroically accomplished.[12]

In Lancashire, too, machine-breaking began a sequence of arms raids and general robberies, and a similar situation existed in Nottinghamshire. Machine-breaking provided a cover for all sorts of criminal activities and an excuse for acts of outrage against the property of individuals. Many a crime was committed and many a private score settled during the Luddite period, it was believed, whilst the authorities were tracking down frame-breakers and looking for culprits amongst the stockingers. The *Nottingham Journal* separated 'Ned Lud's' men from the 'true Luddites'; the former, it suggested, were simply criminals who exploited the existing situation. In the early stages of Luddism selected frames were broken but other private property left untouched; in the later stages thefts were commonplace and the breaking of frames sometimes seemed incidental to the main business. Another feature of frame-breaking in Nottinghamshire, which was peculiar to this area, was the professional nature of the enterprises and the actual employment of men to break machines. This was a further incitement and inducement to the criminals of the area, and undoubtedly prolonged Midlands Luddism at the same time as it was extending crime.[13]

One of the most common features of the disturbances during the Luddite period was that of food riots. There was nothing new about this type of behaviour in times of scarce food and high prices, and economic historians have no difficulty in showing that these conditions prevailed in 1812, the worst—and in Lancashire and Yorkshire the only—year of Luddism. In mid-April there were potato riots in Barnsley and Sheffield, and in the latter case the crowds attacked the local armoury and seized and destroyed several hundred rifles belonging to the militia. The affair, according to General Grey's report to the Home Secretary, had arisen spontaneously and was entirely unconnected with events in the machine-breaking areas of the West Riding further to the north; also the riots, once suppressed, were not followed by other lawless outbreaks. More alarming and more widespread were the mid-April food riots in the cotton country of south Lancashire and north-east Cheshire, with Manchester, Rochdale, Oldham, Bolton, Ashton, Macclesfield, Stockport and Chester all involved. These coincided in time almost exactly with the peak of Lancashire Luddism in Stockport, Middleton and Westhoughton and produced large numbers of prisoners who were tried at the subsequent Chester and Lancaster Assizes, along with men accused of machine-breaking. More food riots occurred throughout England during April, which was both the month of the greatest Luddite crisis on both sides of the Pennines and the month when authorities were most severely plagued by the more conventional problem of food rioting. It is not surprising that the two issues became confused, for the causes of food rioting and Luddism have much in common and it was always possible that what started out as a food riot might, in the current atmosphere, end in an attack upon machinery.

In this context Lancashire poses a particularly acute problem, so much so that the question has been raised of the extent to which Lancashire unrest can reasonably be described as 'authentic Luddism', consisting as it did, in large measure, of

spontaneous riots. But food riots were inextricably bound up
with Luddism in the public mind for several reasons; one was
that informers suggested that there had been Luddite instigation in the fomenting of the troubles, and another was that the
current terminology of Luddism came readily to the lips of
those who were involved in protest movements of other kinds.
The two leaders of the Stockport crowds were men dressed
in women's clothes who described themselves as 'General
Ludd's wives'; Ludd could evidently be expected to rectify
wrongs beyond his usual fields of operation, and where there
was an issue on which women were naturally and traditionally
forward in pressing a popular demand, that for lower food
prices, Ludd's female half assumed leadership of the popular
movement. This happened also in the Leeds corn riots of
August, when 'Lady Ludd', a food rioter using the name of the
supposed leader of the machine-breakers, put herself at the
head of a band of women and boys who rioted in the market-
place and threatened meal-shops in the district. The Stockport
riots of 14 April reached their climax in attacks on the house
and factory of Joseph Goodair, an owner of steam-looms, and
the Middleton battle of 20-21 April between the defenders of
Daniel Burton's steam-loom factory and its numerous hordes
of attackers began as a food riot in Oldham.

After the April upheavals the next round of northern food
riots occurred in August. Again Sheffield was a disturbed
centre, and again it was asserted by the local magistrates that
the disturbances arose entirely as a result of the high price of
flour and had 'no relation to the system that alone is dangerous', that of the secret meetings and oath-takings which were
believed to prevail elsewhere. It was reported from Knottingley that women had almost managed to organise a bread riot
there, and it was a woman, Lady Ludd, who led the corn riots
in Leeds in August. But not even the *Leeds Intelligencer,*
usually alarmist in tone, doubted that the troubles had arisen
on account of high prices, and commentators are agreed that
it was the price of corn at 180s (£9) a quarter which prompted
the troubles.[14]

Meanwhile, in early September, Nottingham, the original centre of Luddism, was itself about to undergo one of its most serious food riots for many years, when the town became the scene of violence and tumult for two days on account of the high price of flour. At the start of the outbreak the rioting women and children were temporarily joined by several of the West Kent Militia stationed in the area, who were allegedly annoyed at being supplied with underweight loaves. But the disturbance was easily put down, as was the potato riot of November, and there was never the least suggestion on either occasion that the food rioting was in any way connected with machine-breaking. After all, Nottingham had experienced its annual food riot and egalitarian behaviour from its crowds for the previous half-century, and so there was nothing new about this sort of event in 1812.[15]

It would appear that the food riots constituted a separate and independent issue, apart from Luddism, connected to it in the sense that food prices and shortages were amongst the grievances experienced by Luddites as well as food rioters and by the fact that angry food rioters might turn Luddite. They were little more than a passing threat to public order in particular places, which they had frequently been throughout the eighteenth century and would remain during the years of an ineffective policing system. But they were a relatively simple and uncomplex problem for the authorities, though complicated at this time by the fact that they were coinciding with the less easily tackled problem of Luddism.

Unquestionably the greatest confusion, for both contemporaries and historians, has arisen from the difficulty involved in separating Luddism from the various political reform movements that were going on concurrently with it, and the greatest mistake has been, in many cases, the failure to draw any distinction between the political and industrial movements. For contemporaries who believed, as many did, that the Luddites had political designs, the obvious leaders with whom to endow the Luddites were the national leaders of the parliamentary reform movement, figures like Major Cartwright, Cobbett, or

Sir Francis Burdett; of these perhaps Burdett was most frequently cited in wild and speculative communications as the man 'to lead the Commonwealth' or alternatively to be 'King of England' after the revolution. The reform leaders were naturally embarrassed by this popular identification of themselves with the exponents of industrial sabotage and direct action, and were always anxious to deny the association. Cartwright was very active promoting the cause of parliamentary reform in all the main Luddite centres in the years 1811-13, in part with the hope of weaning the working classes away from direct action and towards constitutional agitation for reform, but Luddism discredited his cause and the disaffected allegedly looked up to him as their leader in spite of his repeated denunciations of the Luddites and their methods. 'The late rebellious state of Lancashire and Yorkshire', wrote one man in November 1812, 'may chiefly be attributed to the written addresses and inflammatory harangues of Burdett and Cartwright', and even the coolest men on the side of the authorities were guilty of wild statements on the issue of Luddism and parliamentary reform. General Maitland, remarkable for his sanity and careful judgement most of the time, was reporting in late July that petitions for peace and parliamentary reform had just been opened in Lancashire and were being signed by 'those notoriously connected with the late disturbances'. A fortnight later he again reported that the spirit of disaffection remained unabated and that the disaffected were now having meetings for parliamentary reform.

The nature of Luddite disaffection will be discussed at length later, but it seems useful to observe now that Luddism's connection with the parliamentary reform movement was no more than the support that individual Luddites would naturally give to a campaign to reform the political system. It is not surprising that George Mellor, from his condemned cell at York, asked for his name to be added to a petition for reform that was currently being prepared, or that some Luddites in both the Midlands and Lancashire should have later turned their thoughts to parliamentary reform. This is not to say that it was any of their concern as Luddites; the reforming *Leeds Mercury* was scandalised that this association should be voiced, and all reforming leaders did their utmost to deny it.[16]

Two particular cases illustrate well the contemporary and later confusion between Luddism and the political reform movement. One is the case of the '38', sometimes called the '38 Luddites', a group of Manchester reformers who were arrested by Joseph Nadin, deputy constable of Manchester, and tried for administering illegal oaths on the basis of evidence produced by Samuel Fleming, a spy and informer in the pay of Nadin. The proven innocence of the men on the indictment, and the much-publicised opinion of the authorities and a press favourable to them that the men were in fact guilty, constitute a controversy which is not our immediate concern. What is of interest is that the affair should have become part of the story of Luddism in Lancashire. One historian of Manchester, for instance, cites the arrest of the men as evidence that the Luddite conspiracy for breaking machinery had by that time spread to Lancashire. It had, of course, spread to Lancashire several months before the arrest, which is quite irrelevant to Lancashire Luddism anyway. Colonel Ralph Fletcher, the Bolton magistrate who played a very active role against the Luddites, suggested that the Manchester Luddites were actively engaged in raising money for the support of the thirty-eight men, and it was commonly supposed that the oaths with which they were allegedly involved were those which the machine-breakers had themselves taken. In fact the defence of the arrested men was undertaken by Brougham, engaged by Cartwright, who was strongly convinced of the men's innocence concerning oath-taking and Luddite activities. Cartwright's involvement was communicated to the authorities by the informer Yarwood. His suggestion that Cartwright had paid for the men's celebrations on acquittal was intended to lend weight to the idea of the men's guilt and Cartwright's implication in the conspiracy. In fact, it serves now to substantiate the notion of the men's innocence of the charge on which they were indicted; the authorities had done their best to find evidence of guilt by transcribing, annotating, and interpreting all the letters written by the men as prisoners, but they were unable to find anything incriminating. Yet the fact remains that the '38' invariably feature as an integral part of the Luddite story.[17]

Similarly with John Baines, the Halifax hatter; along with his sons, he was convicted on the evidence of spies of administering illegal oaths. He stood trial at the York Assizes in January 1813, together with the men who were convicted of Luddite attacks on mills and the murder of William Horsfall, and Baines inevitably features in accounts of Yorkshire Luddism as the leading figure amongst the Luddites in Halifax. His guilt was proven more to the satisfaction of the authorities than to that of historians; the Crown expected trouble because of the nature of their witnesses, and there is some ground to suppose that they could have been broken and that the defence mismanaged its case. The question of the involvement of Baines in Luddism remains even more open, for the trial revealed nothing. The so-called 'verbal tradition' collected by Frank Peel in the late nineteenth century has Baines as a former Jacobin who patronised and encouraged the Luddites, but the leading modern authority on the question declines to commit himself on the issue of whether political radicals such as Baines were directly involved. It seems probable that Baines and his family were not involved in actual machine-breaking, that as politically orientated working-class intelligentsia they would have serious doubts about the efficacy of machine-breaking as a means of achieving the desired ends, but that as ex-Paineites they were not unhappy to see a blow being struck against authority. But there is no means of knowing whether they properly belong to the Luddite story; this is just one more factor which makes it difficult to tell.[18]

Again, in the trade-union sphere as well as the political one, there is a separate story to tell of working-class industrial activity which sometimes appears to overlap with the Luddite narrative, sometimes appears to have become thoroughly confused with it, and which was none the less a development of much greater antiquity and future than the Luddite phase in industrial relations. The extent of trade-union involvement will be considered in some detail later; it is enough to say now that the fairly well-established trade-union practices that prevailed and the trade-union organisation that existed in the industries troubled by Luddism were further factors which complicated the task of authorities and historians in determining what the Luddites were doing.

Of all the areas associated with Luddism, unquestionably the one which poses the most difficulties for the historian is Lancashire, for there all the many complicating elements were present in abundance; the criminals, the food rioters, the parliamentary reformers and the trade unionists were there in force, activated in part by spies and *agents-provocateurs*, and all of them combining to obscure the phenomenon of machine-breaking which went on in their midst. There was one element that characterised the Luddism of 1812 and separated it from other earlier movements of political and industrial protest, namely the conspiracy over a wide front to attack industrial machinery. Such attacks did occur in Lancashire in 1812, but they were perhaps so very incidental to other matters as to justify the serious raising of the query whether the unrest in Lancashire may be described as 'authentic Luddism'.[19]

So it is necessary now to attempt the essential definition of terms and to say who the Luddites were. For immediate purposes the Luddites were not the Pentrich or Grange Moor rebels, the would-be revolutionaries or the parliamentary reformers, the food rioters or the trade unionists. Nor were they even the Swing rioters or other agricultural or industrial workers who destroyed machinery and practised industrial sabotage as a means of imposing conditions upon employers or making some sort of protest gesture. They were rather the people who broke machinery as a deliberate, calculated policy in a particular historical period, the years 1811-16. It would be possible to examine the phenomenon of machine-breaking in Scotland, in France, or elsewhere, but this study is confined to the English machine-breakers in this period who, for present purposes, are being identified as the Luddites. And it may well be necessary during the course of the examination to ask if the use of one blanket term to cover episodes in different parts of the country does not suggest for Luddism a greater degree of homogeneity and national purpose than it in fact possessed. Perhaps Luddism, like Chartism, is no more than a convenient term which can be as misleading as it is helpful if its regional nature is not emphasised, though it would be useless at this stage to prejudge the issue of how far links were established and maintained between Luddites in different parts of the country and how far they experienced any sense of common purpose in what they did.

To define a subject is not to justify it, and new writing on an old subject is justifiable only if something remains to be said either about the actual events which occurred or the meaning to be placed upon them. Surprisingly for a subject so limited in extent, Luddism has left quite a number of ambiguities about what actually happened. It is not difficult to find accounts of individual incidents which have a fair measure of agreement with each other; it is very difficult to add up the incidents and produce a total which receives general concurrence. It is highly unlikely that historians have still to uncover from diaries, the press, or other sources some previously unnoted Luddite outrage of which we are still in total ignorance, yet it is a difficult task to put together the ones that are known about and to say just how intensively they occurred. And if some apparently basic assembling of fairly elementary material has still to be accomplished, there remains almost infinite scope for disagreement about the meaning of all the incidents which are being assembled. When historians are in agreement about the Luddites, historical controversy will be at an end. It is sound policy to attempt to draw 'only the most tentative conclusions' on many of the main issues arising out of Luddism, even though it is not always possible to resist the temptation to draw conclusions which are something more than tentative.[20]

It would be almost impossible to list all the erroneous statements that have been made about Luddism, that is alleged statements of fact which in no way depend upon interpretation or opinion. A few of these will serve to illustrate the curious things that have been said. The most common confusion has concerned the stocking-frame, the first object of Luddite attention. Though in use since Elizabethan times and basically unchanged in intervening years, it acquired in 1811 a villainous reputation for having come suddenly into existence and having created massive redundancy. The myth of the Luddite who resisted the introduction of machinery was born, and it was nurtured by the behaviour of the Yorkshire Luddites, who really were resisting machinery that created unemployment. Some press accounts blamed only the improvements alleged to have occurred in the stocking-frame, but others went the entire way, to be followed later by historians who wrote of the invention of a new stocking-frame, the violent opposition in Nottingham to the use of stocking-frames (as if the stockinger was demanding the ancient right to use four knitting-needles), and Luddites who went around the countryside destroying machinery wherever they heard it was erected. A slight refinement of this myth has appeared in the official introduction to the Radcliffe Manuscripts, where the Yorkshire Luddites are described as 'followers of the movement in Nottingham against the introduction of machinery into the mills', mills which, unfortunately for the stockingers and their standard of living, did not come into being for a further forty years.

If the fact that the Midlands stockingers had been working stocking-frames for over 200 years at the time of Luddism has led to misunderstanding, so too has the fact that Nottingham Luddism involved two industries, hosiery and lace, which are repeatedly confused. And the extent of the upheavals was a further subject for contemporary misunderstanding which historians have hardly yet managed to clear up. In December 1811, for instance, the *Statesman* carried a report that 20,000 stocking-makers were unemployed, that 900 lace-frames had already been broken at the rate of 20-30 per night (though stocking-frames would have been a more appropriate target for stocking-makers), that corn and hay stacks were being fired throughout Nottinghamshire, and the whole county for twenty miles around the town was full of these ruinous proceedings, which could not be checked. This inaccurate and highly misleading description unfortunately set the tone for many later accounts. It is perhaps not surprising, when accurate information was apparently so difficult to come by and communicate, that the House of Lords Committee of Secrecy should have thought that Liversedge and Heckmondwike, in the heart of the heavy woollen district, which names they encountered in connection with Rawfolds Mill, were in the neighbourhood of the moors dividing Lancashire and Yorkshire. And there is still some tendency to view Yorkshire Luddism as set in a scene from *Wuthering Heights* rather than in the gentler countryside of *Shirley* where it properly belongs. But the differences between Yorkshire and Lancashire, wool and cotton, lace and hosiery, moors and pastures, must be left to emerge rather than be explained in detail to set the record straight.[21]

But if the record should ever be straightened, it would still be difficult to produce a consensus account of Luddism which contained universally acceptable answers to questions about who the Luddites were, why they were Luddites, precisely what they were after, and what exactly they achieved. Some of these remain highly contentious issues, and it is useful briefly to take stock of the historiography of the subject at the present time.

Historians, however great their professionalism and technical competence, remain human beings. We are repeatedly warned that by and large they find in the past what they want to find there, and the factors that influence them in their search are too numerous and complex to warrant discussion here. Yet these factors are particularly important where a subject such as the Luddites is concerned, for it is on this sort of subject that the historian has had particular difficulty in achieving, not objectivity, for this is beyond him, but a recognition of the subjectivity which pervades his work. And so the Luddites have usually been presented as the people we want them to have been and at the same time we have believed that this is what they really were.

Luddites have too frequently had to be either villains or heroes. At least one eminent historian has recently deplored the fact that modern writers are disinclined to apportion blame and guilt and that there are no longer right and wrong sides to be identified. Presumably he is not too unhappy at Luddite historiography, which has always had a generous sprinkling of good men and bad men. A splendid example of the moral judgement that found against the Luddites is that of J. Russell, who in 1906 condemned the Luddites along with other radicals and trade unionists who mistakenly supposed that they could alter society by their agitations, and this in a most detached and scholarly publication which would never believe itself descending to partisan political controversy. The Hammonds, while in no way escaping from their own predispositions, did manage a more balanced outlook in lamenting the conditions that produced Luddism but regretting the means that were chosen to ameliorate them. Their Fabian outlook has in turn brought them heavy censure of late. It has been suggested that the Luddites were given a raw deal by the Hammonds for not being well-behaved trade unionists or parliamentary socialists of a kind who later gave direction to the working-class movement in England and brought it to national respectability. Instead of being judged in the light of how things turned out, they should, it is argued, be judged in their immediate context, for they were living men faced with real and severe problems, not raw material for historians, waiting to be judged as part of some great process. And seen in this way they have been adjudged men of heroic stature and noble achievement. We are now almost back amongst the cowboys and Indians, our good men and bad men, with the traditional roles reversed, the upholders of law rather than the law-breakers, the employers rather than the workers, taking

on the part of the villains, and the Luddites filling the role
of the virtuous.[22]

Naturally opinions have changed on just about all aspects
of Luddism. To the authorities of the day its causes were
not a matter of prime importance; they saw the problem as
one of law and order and their main concern was to suppress
Luddism and punish the evil-doers for the wrongs committed.
It was left to critics of the government to suggest that an equal
concern should be the matters which gave rise to Luddism
and that a more constructive approach to the problem might
be to investigate the causes with a view to eliminating them,
rather than simply to deal with the outward manifestations of
the discontent. Historians have, of course, rectified this situation and, seeing the explanation of causes as just as much
their task as the description of events, have investigated the
causes of Luddism at some length; at too great a length, perhaps, for some who feel that we are now in danger of failing
to see the wood for the trees. We have spent so much time
accumulating statistics and basing conclusions upon them that
we have failed to appreciate the more basic, fundamental point
that Luddism represented 'the crisis point in the abrogation of
paternalist legislation, and in the imposition of the political
economy of laissez faire upon, and against the will and con-
science of, the working people'. We should take a broader,
more imaginative view of the causes of Luddism and not see
it in too narrow an economic and historical context, though
the Luddites themselves must be seen in precisely this sort
of context.[23]

On the question of Luddite aims we have now completed
a curious full circle. Whereas many contemporaries were convinced that the industrial grievances of the Luddites were only
symptomatic of a deeper discontent and that their industrial
activities were merely the forerunner of much more serious
political activities which would culminate in revolution, it has
been the main task of the historian to deny that the Luddites
had any such intentions and to place them firmly in an industrial context, with industrial grievances and industrial aims.

Page 33: (*above*) John Wood's cropping-shop, Longroyd Bridge, Huddersfield, where George Mellor worked and Luddite coups were planned; (*below*) the 40lb handshears which the croppers fought to retain

Page 34: Locations of machine-breaking in six counties, 1811-16

And that was Luddite orthodoxy until the nineteenth century alarmists and sensationalists found surprising support for their views and interpretations from E. P. Thompson, who felt that the Luddites, judged as mere discontented workers, were receiving less than justice. They have now re-emerged, still with their economic discontent, but also with the alternative morality and alternative political system towards which they were groping, some more vaguely than others. If the Luddites were heroic figures worthy of lionisation, it follows that their opponents were right to be frightened of them and to treat them as seriously as they did, and the extremist interpretations of partially informed and panic-stricken magistrates are now acquiring a belated justification in the most unexpected of places.[24]

Similarly, we are being urged to change our opinions radically about the nature of Luddite achievements. If contemporaries thought that Luddism had any consequences, they measured them in terms of the harmful effects that machine-breaking had on industrial growth, frightening away capital from particular areas and retarding mechanisation in industries which needed it. They believed that the Luddites had misjudged completely their own interests and that their behaviour could have nothing but detrimental results for them; machine-breaking brought them no profits and, in so far as working-class prosperity derived from industrial prosperity, it damaged their prospects for the future. It eventually became clear that the damaging consequences of Luddism for industrial development had been exaggerated, but the objective appraisal of Darvall could find no working-class gains from Luddism save the indirect ones which came as a result of reforms a couple of decades later, reforms which, it might be argued, owed their existence in part to the deficiencies in the old system that Luddism had exposed.

Perhaps the first major attempt to suggest that the Luddites had appraised their situation realistically and acted rationally and profitably was made by E. J. Hobsbawm, who suggested collective bargaining by riot as a feasible alterna-

C

tive to more orthodox trade unionism in the years of the Combination Laws. The problem was to show that the collective bargaining had actually achieved something and had been a worthwhile enterprise. The view that it had was later advanced with great force when it was suggested that Luddism represented a more realistic assessment of the economic situation than the employers were showing and that the successes of the Luddites were to be measured in currency other than a purely economic one, that is their contribution to working-class consciousness through their very willingness to act illegally and challenge society. A dispassionate observer who needs to see achievements in some measurable currency continues to have difficulty in accepting that the Luddites bettered themselves, their successors, or their industries, through their efforts. It is difficult to see how they contributed positively to thinking on the problems of any of the industries in which they were involved, and there must still be a strong inclination to see their thinking and methods as irrelevant to anything other than an immediate satisfaction of a sense of grievance deeply felt. They were in no sense moving towards the thinking or techniques which were eventually able to strengthen their own bargaining powers in the economic battle or give them power to wield inside the state.[25]

And if it is necessary to re-pose all the fundamental questions about Luddism and the Luddites, it is equally necessary to ask what means are now available to help ensure that these questions shall be given accurate answers. On the official side the documentation is vast, with the enormous bulk of material in the Public Record Office being supplemented in recent years by the papers of the Lord-Lieutenant of the West Riding, Earl Fitzwilliam, and the magistrate most active in suppressing Yorkshire Luddism, Joseph Radcliffe of Huddersfield. On the Luddite side there is, of course, very little; by the very nature of their existence the Luddites were precluded from keeping records of their activities, and it was only after individuals were taken into captivity that they contributed to the written record of their enterprises, through depositions and confessions. The events of Luddism are well enough known, but it has recently been suggested that much work remains for the local historian in the provincial centres before its mysteries are properly cleared up. It must still be felt that the local stages are being filled by names rather than by people and there is much that the historian would like to know about the individuals who were involved in Luddism, their motives, their activities, and their feelings.

Some of this can be discovered by reference to what has been described as 'oral tradition', stories handed down by word of mouth and recorded by such people as Frank Peel who attempted to check and confirm much that was told to him before producing his account of Yorkshire Luddism in the 1880s. This kind of evidence, lively and entertaining as it can undoubtedly be, is, however, some of the most difficult to handle, and there is a danger that it might be given a weighting and importance beyond its merits. Peel did perhaps attempt to check his material against the files of the *Leeds Mercury*, but that did not prevent him from making a great number of mistakes in his facts and his interpretation, and he is not entitled to be considered a primary source of the reliability that has been accorded him. But even if this sort of account could not be proved in parts erroneous and misleading, it would still be undesirable for a historian to accept the authenticity of a story on the ground that it was 'according to tradition'. Traditions are often notoriously corrupted versions of the original, and traditions relating to Luddism have doubtless been determined by what men have chosen to remember and hand down rather than by what actually occurred at the time. 'Popular legend' might have given pride of place to the great hammers used by the Yorkshire Luddites in their midnight maraudings, but 'popular legend' is not necessarily the stuff of which good history is made, however entertaining it might be for its own sake.[26]

Whether much new information is still recoverable must be a matter of doubt, and until more is known the problem is to make proper use of the information that is available. The

great figures in Luddite historiography, the Hammonds and
Darvall, looked at the source material and reached their conclusions on the basis of what they could show to be so from
the records. Speculations and accusations which could not be
justified or substantiated by the documents were discounted,
and in consequence these historians have been accused of
writing unimaginatively. This 'failure of the historical imagination', which has allegedly afflicted other and more recent
writers is, indeed, a problem in interpreting material which
is usually not so complete as its user would wish, but the use
of the imagination, while a necessary part of the historian's
technique, constitutes a comparable problem if it leads to
flights of pure fancy. The hypothesis of the imaginative historian must fall some way short of the fiction of the novel-
writer if it is to be a useful working basis for future research.
What any reassessment of Luddism now involves is, in fact,
a further look at the issues and traditional accounts in the
light of E. P. Thompson's *Making of the English Working
Class,* for early nineteenth century English history can never
be the same again since the publication of this work.[27]

1 *Nottingham Review,* 20 December 1811; Blackner, J. *History
   of Nottingham* (1815) pp 401-3; Hobsbawm, E. J. and Rudé,
   G. *Captain Swing* (1969) pp 17, 19 and jacket
2 Hobsbawm, E. J. *The Machine Breakers, Past and Present*
   (1952) 1
3 Hobsbawm, E. J. *The Machine Breakers*; the term 'blackleg'
   in fact belongs to the second half of the century, before which
   time different local terms were employed, eg 'nobs' in Scotland;
   McCallum, D. *Old and New Glasgow* (1890) p 7
4 Hobsbawm, E. J. *The Machine Breakers*; Henson, G. *History
   of the Framework Knitters* (1831) pp 95-6; Hammond, J. L.
   and B. *The Skilled Labourer* (1919) p 226; *Nottingham
   Journal,* 3 November 1787; Rudé, G. *The Crowd in History*
   (1964) pp 66-77
5 Hobsbawm, E. J. *The Machine Breakers*; Baines, E. *History
   of the Cotton Manufacture in Great Britain* (1835) pp 151,
   158
6 Wadsworth, A. P. and Mann, J. D. L. *The Cotton Trade and*

Industrial Lancashire, 1600-1780 (1931) p 101; Rudé, G. *The Crowd in History* pp 71-3

7   Wadsworth, A. P. and Mann, J. D. L. *The Cotton Trade and Industrial Lancashire, 1600-1780* (1931) p 353; *Leeds Mercury, 25 January 1812; Thompson, E. P. *The Making of the English Working Class* (1963) p 525, quotes Fitzwilliam MSS F45d for Huddersfield incident

8   Wadsworth, A. P. and Mann, J. D. L. *The Cotton Trade and Industrial Lancashire, 1600-1780,* pp 302, 375, 380, 478-81; Bythell, D. *The Handloom Weavers* (1969) p 74

9   Rudé, G. *The Crowd in History,* p 85; *Leeds Intelligencer,* 7 December 1812

10 HO (Home Office papers) 42/118, Crich correspondent to HO, 5 December 1811; Fitzwilliam MSS 45/140; HO 42/129, Fitzwilliam to Maitland, 2 November 1812; Radcliffe MSS 126/114

11 *Leeds Intelligencer,* 13 July 1812; *Leeds Mercury,* 5 December 1812; HO 42/130, Confession of James Hay, 14 December 1812; Mayall, J. *Annals of Yorkshire* (1859) pp 239-240

12 HO 42/127, Allison to HO, 15 September 1812; Fitzwilliam MSS 46/94; Thompson, E. P. *The Making . . . .* p 572

13 HO 42/119, Brief Statement of Transactions in the County and Town of Nottingham; HO 42/153, Enfield to HO, 14 October 1816; *Nottingham Journal,* 10 January 1812; HO 42/117, Coldham to HO, 13 December 1811; Sutton, J. F. *The Date Book of Nottingham, 1750-1850* (1852) p 334

14 *Leeds Mercury,* 18, 25 April 1812; Fitzwilliam MSS 45/127, 128; HO 42/122, Grey to HO, 18 April 1812; Thompson, E. P. *The Making . . . .* pp 565-6; *Manchester Mercury,* 21 April 1812; *Manchester Commercial Advertiser,* 21 April 1812; Parsons, E. *History of Leeds* (1834) p 74; *Leeds Mercury,* 15, 22 August 1812; HO 42/125, Maitland to HO, 22 August 1812; *Leeds Mercury,* 15 August 1812; *Leeds Intelligencer,* 24 August 1812

15 *Nottingham Review,* 11 September 1812; *Nottingham Journal,* 7 November 1812

16 HO 40/1, 'Ned Ludd' to Mr Smith, undated; HO 42/127, details of persons committed at York; Miller, N. C. 'John Cartwright and Radical Reform, 1808-19', *English Historical Review,* LXXXIII, 1968; HO 42/129, Higgins to HO, 2 November 1812; HO 42/125, Maitland to HO, 20 July 1812; HO 42/127, 5 August 1812; Thompson, E. P. *The Making . . . .* p 602; *Leeds Mercury,* 19 September 1812

17 Bruton, F. A. *Short History of Manchester and Salford* (1927)

pp 169-70; HO 42/124, Fletcher to HO, 30 June 1812; Miller, N. C. 'John Cartwright and Radical Reform 1808-19'; HO 40/2, Lloyd to HO, 16 October 1812; HO 42/129, verbatim copies of extracts from prisoners' letters

18   HO 42/129, Hobhouse to HO, 29 November 1812; Peel, F. *The Risings of the Luddites* (1880) p 24; Thompson, E. P. *The Making* .... p 590

19   Ibid pp 565-6

20   Ibid p 575

21   *Leeds Mercury*, 23 November 1811; Astle, W. ed *History of Stockport* (1922) p 7; Sykes, D. F. E. *History of Huddersfield and its vicinity* (1898) p 273; Stirling, A. M. W. *Annals of a Yorkshire House* (1911); *Statesman* article quoted in *Leeds Mercury*, 21 December, 1811; Report of House of Lords Committee of Secrecy, July 1812; Rudé, G. *The Crowd in History* p 86

22   Taylor, A. J. P. *The Observer*, 27 July 1969; Russell, J. 'The Luddites', *Transactions of the Thoroton Society*, 1906; Hammond, J. L. & B. *The Skilled Labourer* (1919); Thompson, E. P. *The Making of the English Working Class*.

23   Ibid p 543

24   eg Darvall, F. O. *Popular Disturbances and Public Order in Regency England* (1934); Thompson, E. P. *The Making* ....

25   Darvall, F. O. *Popular Disturbances* .... pp 215-17; Hobsbawm, E. J. *The Machine Breakers*; Thompson, E. P. *The Making* .... pp 550-1, 601

26   Introduction to fourth edition of Peel, F. *The Risings of the Luddites,* by E. P. Thompson (1969) p XV; eg Thompson, E. P. *The Making* .... pp 557, 559

27   Ibid p 577 and postscript to 2nd edition

Chapter Two

THE CAUSES OF LUDDISM

THE CAUSES OF Luddism are a problem which has exercised many minds and produced many different answers. It appeared for a time that agreement had very largely been reached on the issue, but the 'otiose "economist" explanation' has recently been rejected and in its place substituted an interpretation which places Luddism less in the context of the French and American wars and more in the context of the rise of laissez-faire.[1]

Contemporaries had plenty to say on this as on other aspects of Luddism and many were far from accepting any 'otiose "economist" explanation' of what was happening. Something more than the distresses of the time, suggested the *Leeds Intelligencer,* was the moving cause of these conspiracies, and the House of Lords Committee of Secrecy, attempting to summarise and interpret the enormous correspondence that was building up in Home Office files, a task on which they are deserving of no little sympathy, listed the alleged causes of Luddism but gave it as the opinion of many that some Luddite views extended to revolutionary measures of the most dangerous description; the end purpose of it all, they believed, was still to be revealed. Even General Maitland, who a few weeks later was assessing the situation much more soberly, believed, after his early contacts with Lancashire magistrates and informers, in the existence of a combination to overcome all legal authority, which he saw as 'the real groundwork' of the

existing state of affairs. The precise nature of this combination
and conspiracy will be considered later. J. Lloyd of Stockport,
an indefatigable pursuer of Luddites throughout 1812, was
prepared, in the early days in February, to believe that the
bad spirit was being kept up by a few desperate characters
from Ireland, but his later experiences no doubt caused him
to modify these views. Others held to the view that the country's
rebellious state was to be attributed chiefly to the 'written
addresses and inflammatory harangues of Burdett and Cartwright', giving to these reform leaders an influence they could
not have imagined they possessed and a following of disciples
hardly congenial to them.[2]

The Duke of Newcastle reported that foreign agency was
strongly suspected of being the instigation of the trouble; his
own ground for supporting this notion was that Luddite affairs
were conducted with very great ability, for he accepted the
view, now seriously challenged, that the working classes were
not themselves capable of this degree of efficiency and organisation. Almost inevitably at this time, France was believed
by some to be behind the plot to disrupt the British war effort.
A threatening letter received by a Huddersfield manufacturer
contained the 'information' that the Luddites were hoping for
assistance from the French Emperor, and there were people
ready enough to believe that this was actually forthcoming.
According to the *Leeds Intelligencer,* Luddites were receiving
eighteen shillings per week on being enrolled or 'twisted in',
which money was being transmitted from France. As far as
Nottingham was concerned, stories were frequently circulated that men with French accents had been seen in the town,
their purpose being presumably to distribute the money necessary to keep the Luddites at work; according to one source
it was costing Napoleon £4,000 a week to carry out his policy
of industrial sabotage. This and other stories were investigated
by Conant and Baker, two London police officers who were
sent up to Nottingham by the Home Office, but they could
find no substance in the rumours. It was only the weak and
corrupt, said the *Leeds Mercury,* who would suggest that

the riots in Nottinghamshire owed their origin to French gold; the stockingers were much too loyal and patriotic to riot for anything other than sound, domestic reasons while their country was at war.[3]

Perhaps the wildest and most amusing conspiracy theory of them all was that which Gravener Henson, the Nottingham trade-union leader, advanced to Francis Place a number of years later: he suggested that Luddism was a put-up job by the government of the day to give it an excuse for grinding the people under the heel of military despotism. It is certain that Henson knew far too much about the origins of Luddism to permit him seriously to believe a notion of this kind; the likelihood is that this comic attempt at writing a bit of Whig history was meant to pull the leg of Francis Place, who recorded it with apparent gravity as a piece of serious comment.[4]

The more mundane, pedestrian approach, which looks at Luddism against a background of trade depression, unemployment, low wages and high prices, merits more serious consideration. That witnesses before the 1812 Committee on the working of the Orders in Council should have unanimously regarded working-class distress as the most acute they had known makes this an obvious starting-point for an examination of the causes of Luddism. Before any machine-breaking started in the North of England, the Home Secretary received letters and petitions from Bolton in November 1811, complaining of high food prices and the low wages of the working classes and predicting the fearful consequences that would follow any further rise in the price of grain or potatoes should that be unaccompanied by an equivalent rise in wages. It was just this situation which developed through the winter and spring of 1812.

Six months later the Bolton magistrate, R. A. Fletcher, an inveterate hater of the Luddites and an unscrupulous hounder of them, was reporting that the price of oatmeal and potatoes had doubled and that there would be great distress among working people until a plentiful harvest rectified the situation.

And Fletcher was a great exponent of the revolutionary conspiracy theory of Luddism. Similarly, General Maitland from
Manchester found in May 1812 a considerable degree of distress occasioned by the high price of provisions. He suggested
that here the usual retail price of potatoes had trebled of
late, with wages falling by almost the same proportion as
prices had risen; not surprisingly he expected a great sourness
and irritability to exist in these circumstances, though he was
still, at this stage, viewing these factors as aids to 'the pro-
moters of any Revolutionary system' rather than as causes in
themselves of the prevalent disturbances.[5]

From Yorkshire there came a clearer appraisal of the importance of high prices in determining the situation. Lord
Fitzwilliam's magistrates repeatedly emphasised to him the
distress caused by the high and increasing price of provisions;
it was the pressure of starvation and the 'calamitous priva-
tions of the poorer classes' which were producing the present
unrest, and the solution of the problem, it was suggested, lay
with the harvest and with trade, not with the magistrates. This
was official support for the view expressed by one witness at
the York Assizes in July, which was 'If there be a good trade
and meal come down, Ned Ludd will die', and no less a
person than General Maitland himself was happily anticipating
the beneficial influence of a good harvest when he wrote from
Wakefield on 12 September. As in Lancashire, it was the sud-
den advances in the price of flour and potatoes which caused
the greatest devastation, Colonel Clay reported to his superiors
on 23 March; and one factor which was given particular
emphasis in a letter from Sheffield was that oats had doubled
in price, which had helped to put many hundreds of thousands
in a state of desperation; the importance of oats to the northern
diet, it was suggested, was a fact not known to those in London
and the south. It would be possible to quote endlessly from
historians on this theme or from annalists such as Frank Peel
who recorded from Heckmondwike in the Spen Valley that
wheat prices there reached 155s (£7.75) per quarter in 1812,
a figure never exceeded before or afterwards, and that four

poor rates of three shillings (15p) in the pound were exacted in the one year to help meet the attendant distress.[6]

From Nottingham a very similar picture emerges. In May 1812 an ironical correspondent suggested in the local press that the present troubles might be cured if doctors would only get together to find out how appetite might be eliminated; an emergency relief committee was currently distributing 10,000 sixpenny tickets which could be exchanged at food shops. Prices locally were never higher in the period 1792-1829, apart from flour which was dearer only in the years of famine, 1800 and 1801, and there was no reluctance to accept the verdict, later recorded by William Felkin, that hunger and misery were the basic causes of Luddism. Through the winter of 1811-12, he wrote, the almost universal cry was 'give us work at any price—half a loaf is better than no bread'.[7]

If social tension can be expected in years following bad harvests and in times of high food prices, then 1812 was, by universal agreement among historians, a year of inevitable social tension. The Treasury Solicitors might argue, in preparing a brief against men charged with administering unlawful oaths, that the recent alarming outrages owed their origin to a deep-laid scheme to overthrow the government and not to any local circumstances created by the lowness of wages or dearness of provisions, but the relevant government departments were kept sufficiently well-informed of the importance of local circumstances to know that wages and prices were matters of the highest consequence.[8]

The 'otiose "economist's" explanation' of Luddism lays great stress on the dislocation to trade caused by the French and American wars, Napoleon's continental system, the retaliatory Orders in Council, and the later American interdict on trade with Britain, all of which hit particularly the manufacturing industries, which had their main overseas markets in French-occupied Europe and America. When the American blow fell on top of the earlier ones the manufacturing industries were almost prostrated, and opponents of the government did not hesitate to point out the connection between its foreign and naval policies and the domestic disturbances it was facing. Fitzwilliam, responsible for the preservation of law and order in the West Riding, firmly advised the ending of the Orders in Council; put the manufacturers to work again, he wrote, and outrage and conspiracy would die away, for they were assuredly the offspring of distress and unemployment. If the merchants could be made active again it would do more good than all the activities of the magistrates in stopping the trouble. And the Lord-Lieutenant's officials and advisers supplied him with ample statistics to support the case that they continued to press upon him; of about a million pounds-worth of woollen cloth in the hands of merchants associated with the Leeds Cloth Hall, mostly intended for the American market and accumulating since October 1810; of a woollen trade able to employ only half its usual members, and half of these underemployed and earning six shillings (30p) a week in contrast with the ten shillings (50p) or ten-and-sixpence of the fully employed and the seventeen shillings (85p) that was the previous norm. This was the sort of detail that caused historians of the industry to write of 1812 opening with bank failures and bankruptcies, of firms collapsing while their employees were faced with the sight of wheat soaring to famine prices. It was the 1812 experience that caused the Leeds reports of January 1813 to discuss the ending of Luddism and the happier state of the countryside in terms of the improving state of trade, the general advance in the price of wool, the favourable turn in coarse and fine cloth, the vast amount of orders received from America, and the prospects of a very prosperous spring.[9]

By June 1812 General Maitland was beginning to see prevailing economic conditions in Lancashire as something more than a means of facilitating the work of would-be revolutionaries. He admitted that he knew of no instance of a considerable stagnation of trade accompanied by the high price of provisions where some disturbance akin to Luddism had not been the result. This was to admit the existing commercial situation as a first cause of the trouble. In February the Home

Secretary had been warned by a Manchester commercial house that prices, and thereby wages, for manufactured goods must be got up since 'there is a point beyond which human nature cannot bear', and even R. A. Fletcher of Bolton believed that the raising of wages was a priority in dealing with the situation. On 4 July Sir Oswald Mosley was writing that the revocation of the Orders in Council had already given a great stimulus to trade in Manchester, and that all would be well if the government did not act too harshly against those responsible for the disturbances, for 'work is all they want and that they are now likely to procure'.[10]

By December Maitland showed himself a thorough convert to the new principles when he reported the salutary effects of the 'good Russian news'; long days were being worked in cotton, people were 'full of business', and all would go well if this economic climate continued. At the same time Captain Macdougal of the Stirlingshire Militia was reporting from Stalybridge that the town was now all quiet since the cotton masters were working long hours and the spinners were receiving higher wages. The disturbances, it was implied, had been the consequence of the unfavourable economic conditions during the earlier part of the year.[11]

The hosiery trade needed only the interference in foreign trade by enemy and government action to precipitate the crisis that was bound to come eventually in view of the unhealthy condition of the industry. The many grievances of the stockingers, their underpayment, the impositions they had to tolerate, such as frame-rents and deductions for wastage of materials, or the readiness of manufacturers to employ un-apprenticed hands, derived essentially from an over-populated, over-producing industry. It continued to be organised on a domestic basis and failed to experience organisational or technological change because an abundant labour supply and the existence of the frame-renting system provided disincentives to the application of power and the transfer to factory production.

This stagnant, over-subscribed industry, which, along with its subsidiaries, absorbed almost the entire working force of

Nottingham, had become by 1811 very dependent on overseas markets. It was estimated that almost half the hosiery and perhaps three-quarters of the lace trade was with American and continental markets, and this almost dried up through 1811. From 1809, when the serious consequences of war for trade really began to be felt, until the outbreak of Luddism, the industry slumped and wages fell by an estimated one-third. It was later claimed that the average wage of the framework-knitter before the outbreak of Luddism was about 7s 3d (36p) per week, which is in line with the statement of a silk-stocking knitter, from a highly paid branch, that he was earning 12s (60p) in 1812. Luddism in Nottinghamshire arose initially out of a wage dispute, for the frames broken in March 1811 belonged to underpaying hosiers who were attempting to stimulate their business by lowering production costs. It seems not unreasonable to argue that if wages had not fallen the arguments about cut-ups and the many other grievances that the stockingers possessed would not have been heard, and that these other issues were as much the consequence of the early rounds of frame-breaking as a first cause; manufacturers had themselves condemned the cut-up production which was later to loom so large in the workmen's arguments.[12]

Before machine-breaking had spread beyond the Midland counties the *Leeds Mercury* argued that the cause of riotous disposition was not confined to Nottinghamshire; it existed in almost all the manufacturing areas in the kingdom. It was only in Nottinghamshire and neighbouring areas that the rioting had actually broken out, though later events were to provide some justification for the paper's early expressed opinion. When the disturbances did spread to other manufacturing areas they did, however, remain localised, and it is the conditions prevailing in particular branches of particular trades that must now be examined as a further part of the explanation of why Luddism occurred.[13]

Any investigation of the causes of Luddism must inevitably concern itself with asking how far Luddism was a matter of resistance to mechanisation and technical innovation, for the

Luddites have achieved their historical fame and lay reputation for their supposed stand on this issue. It has already been
suggested that as far as the first Luddite machine-breakers,
those in Nottinghamshire, were concerned, machines were
almost incidental to their purpose and were not themselves
an object of workers' hostility. This point can now be taken
further. The grievances of the men were many and varied; they
concerned wage-reductions, truck payments and other devices
used by some employers to defraud them over wages, the
employment of 'colts' or unapprenticed workmen inside the
trade, and, most recently, the manufacture of 'cut-ups' and
other inferior articles which were allegedly bringing their trade
into disrepute. The men were not, as has recently been suggested, concerned chiefly to attack the system of frame-renting,
though they were undoubtedly interested in reducing frame-
rents. On the principle of renting they maintained a curiously
ambivalent attitude, arising in part from the desire of many
men themselves to become frame-owners and rentiers and in
part from an acceptance that frame-rent was part of the traditional property right which should go unchallenged, whatever
was in practice being done to individual frames.[14]

Machinery was selected for breaking because it was employed on the kind of manufacture that the workmen were
anxious to ban or because it belonged to employers who were
allegedly guilty of one of the practices against which the men
protested. In an industry where mechanisation had prevailed
since Elizabethan times and framesmiths and machine operators were themselves concerned with improvements to existing models, it would have been meaningless to have thought
in terms of resistance to machinery as such, and the contemporary commentators and later chroniclers who so
caricatured the Nottinghamshire Luddites betrayed a total
ignorance of the hosiery and lace industries. It was probably
the Lord-Lieutenant of Nottinghamshire, the Duke of Newcastle, who first put in circulation the story of new machinery
which was creating redundancy amongst the stockingers as
it could be operated by women. Unfortunately the House of

Lords Committee of Secrecy gave the view their seal of approval in their report of July 1812, and Lord Byron too, in his moving and much-quoted speech, talked of men 'sacrificed to improvements in mechanism'. The view became fully established, though founded on a myth. Neither Luddite declarations nor the more official statements of the trade unions made reference to any such machinery or any such grievance, and the *Nottingham Review* had made a valiant though abortive attempt to scotch the rumours by stating, quite plainly, in December 1811, that there was no new machinery in Nottingham or its neighbourhood against which the workmen were directing their fury. If the workmen disliked certain machines it was because of the use to which they were being put, not because they were machines or because they were new.[15]

When machine-breaking was extended to the West Riding and to the woollen cloth trade the situation was quite different, and the cropper it was who began to act up to the popular notion of what machine-breaking was all about. Workmen involved in the finishing of cloth, the croppers who raised the nap with teazles and then cut it with an enormous pair of shears, had long been fighting a battle, in some areas with great success, against the two machines which were threatening to eliminate their role in the making of cloth. These were the gig-mill, which was a set of mechanically-operated rollers for raising the nap, and the shearing-frame, a rather crude device which simply set up the existing hand shears on a power-operated frame. The history of the previous twenty years leaves no doubt about the campaign waged by the croppers against the gig-mill and the shearing-frame, and when machine-breaking began in Yorkshire in January 1812 it represented the culmination of this campaign. The firm concerned, Oates, Wood and Smithson of Leeds, unhesitatingly attributed the attack to their having of late erected machinery for the finishing of cloth. And the various threatening letters sent by Luddites and received by machine-owners made it perfectly clear that the Luddite campaign was intended 'to

Page 51: The stocking-frame, an Elizabethan invention

December 23, 1811.

WHEREAS

A most violent Attack was made about 8 o'clock last Night, on the House of Mr. JOHN BRENTNALL, at Locko Grange, in the County of Derby, by Eight or more Persons, two of whom with their Faces blacked & armed with Pistols, entered the House, but in consequence of the spirited Resistance of the Family, retired without effecting their villainous purposes.

One of the Men about five feet nine inches high and broad set, is supposed to have his Head, Face, and Neck much injured in a struggle; and another Man about six feet high is supposed to be wounded by a Bill Hook; the other Men who did not enter the House, as far as could be distinguished from the darkness of the night, appeared to be above the common size.

A REWARD OF

FIFTY POUNDS

Has been offered by his Royal Highness the Prince Regent on the Conviction of EACH PERSON concerned in any Outrages of the above nature, and a free Pardon in case the Person giving such information as may lead to the Conviction shall be liable to be prosecuted for the same.

(J. Drewry, Printer, Derby.)

Page 52: Handbill offering a reward

stop the Shearing Frames and Gig Mills' and that hostility was directed against this machinery as such.[16]

In south Lancashire it is by no means clear that the hand-loom weavers were carrying out a serious campaign against the introduction of steam looms which they had any realistic prospect or even hope of achieving. On the other hand, there was some feeling against the steam looms in 1812, and the hostility of the Lancashire Luddite was said to be directed against the new machinery because it was new machinery and because it appeared to pose a threat to his existence. It was the declared intention of the Luddites, as seen in threatening letters and later depositions, to destroy the machinery used in steam-loom weaving, and it was the innovators such as Radcliffe, Goodair and Marsland of Stockport and the owners of the improved looms at Westhoughton who were the victims of Luddite attacks. There is no doubt then that the 'anti-machinery' element popularly associated with the Luddites was present in both Yorkshire and Lancashire. and it is the context and arguments of the Northern machine-breakers which must now be examined.[17]

The making of woollen cloth in Yorkshire was, at the beginning of the nineteenth century, essentially a domestic rather than a factory industry, though the scribbling-miller who prepared the wool, the clothier who wove it into cloth, and the merchant who disposed of it would be operating through workshop units rather than individual workmen's homes. Towards the end of the eighteenth century some firms were bringing various processes together under one roof and establishing the new factory unit; such were Gotts of Leeds or Brookes of Honley, Huddersfield, though in the latter case spinning and weaving were still put out, with the mills looking after the scribbling, finishing, dyeing, and warehousing stages. The movement towards a factory system threatened to eliminate the master clothier, whose workshop would contain enough spinning jennies and looms to employ few outside his own family; it also antagonised the cloth finishers or dressers, the croppers, when the factory owners began to

D

experiment with powered machinery for the finishing of cloth. It is known that the gig-mill, an ancient device outlawed by legislation of Edward VI's reign, had been introduced into Bradley Mills, Huddersfield, before 1784, and nearly all the Huddersfield witnesses who appeared before the 1806 committee of enquiry had had experience of gig-mills, either as croppers operating the machines, or as fine-drawers who had mended the cloth dressed by gigs. In all cases the workmen expressed opposition to the use of gigs. This opposition had taken a very violent form in the West Country industry in the last years of the eighteenth century and the early years of the nineteenth, and in the much nearer Leeds the croppers had successfully resisted the declared intention of Leeds cloth merchants in 1791 to introduce the gig-mill. When the Oatlands Mill was fired in January 1812 the *Leeds Mercury* recalled that about thirteen years previously a similar mill erected at Holbeck had been burnt to the ground by the local populace.

In fact so powerful did the Institution, the croppers' organisation, become that it successfully resisted all attempts to introduce the gigs in the Leeds area for many more years; when, in 1813, the powerful Benjamin Gott was working 48 jennies and 144 looms and doing his own finishing, that work was still being done by hand. Other merchants who had not acquired their own finishing shops were still sending their cloth to the Halifax or Huddersfield areas where the power of the Institution was much less and the gig-mill had come into fairly general use. Thus the pattern of technological application varied according to the area and was determined in large measure by the strength of the croppers' organisation in a particular area.[18]

Similarly the pattern of distribution of the shearing-frame was an uneven one. A shearing-frame had been first patented in 1787 and a further one in 1794; it is known that the shearing-frame was introduced at Bradley Mills in 1800, withdrawn, and reintroduced in 1803 when it caused offence amongst the croppers. At least two other firms had shearing-frames at

the time of the 1806 enquiry, and their use was extended
between then and the Luddite outbreaks of 1812. William
Horsfall, of Marsden, Huddersfield, assassinated by Luddites
in April 1812, was said to have worked shearing-frames for
seven years and to have brought them to a state of great
perfection; Foster's machinery at Horbury, near Wakefield,
destroyed in that month, was also said to have been at work
for several years, while William Cartwright, the attack on
whose mill at Rawfolds constituted the major incident in
Yorkshire Luddism, had begun to experiment in cloth-finishing
by water-power in 1809. It is not true to suggest that the
inventions that provoked Yorkshire Luddism were of immediate novelty, but though the hostility was well-established
it had not, except in Leeds, reached the point of violent
resistance before 1812; it was the more extensive use of the
machinery in the context of commercial depression created by
the wars that produced the violence of that year. And, ironi-
cally, the Leeds area, where resistance had previously been
most violent and organisation of opposition most complete,
remained in 1812 an area of little activity. Although the
factory system was more strongly established there than in
other cloth centres, mechanised cloth-finishing had been kept
out by the power of the croppers and there were hardly any
offensive machines to break in 1812. Conversely, where
mechanisation was furthest advanced and where the men were
at their weakest in terms of organisation, violence occurred, a
contrast which probably suggested to the croppers outside the
Leeds area illusory ideas of the power of organised resistance
and their own ability to benefit by it. If it was the areas where
the croppers were least organised that experienced the greatest violence of Luddism, it was also the remoter areas, where
the authorities had the greatest difficulty in effectively policing
their territory, and the pattern which can be detected in
Yorkshire was one with which the town and county magistrates of Nottinghamshire were already well familiar.[19]

The hostile reception given by the working classes in the
1770s to the inventions of Hargreaves and Arkwright, which

revolutionised spinning processes in the cotton industry, is a familiar story of the Industrial Revolution. The Lancashire spinsters were forerunners of the classic Luddite who resisted mechanisation because it threatened his existence. But it was this machinery, according to one Manchester newspaper, that had raised the cotton trade from nothing to the staple trade and leading manufacture of the kingdom; having accepted the machinery, the working classes knew their own interests too well to destroy the means by which they lived, for without it 'the trade would instantly wing its flight from this district'. The mechanisation of spinning had produced for the hand-loom weavers years of unexampled prosperity which lasted until the end of the eighteenth century, after which time their trade became the 'refuge of the surplus numbers from nearly all other trades' and wages began their long, almost continuous fall in the same way as they did in the hosiery trade after 1809. In the period of declining prosperity from 1799 to the outbreak of Luddism in 1812, the handloom weavers were concerned particularly with wages, and their efforts were directed towards parliamentary regulation for their trade and the achievement of a minimum wage. Unlike the croppers during this same period, they did not direct their attention particularly to newly invented machinery. The exception to this occurred in 1792, when Grimshaw's factory at Manchester, containing twenty-four of Cartwright's patent power-looms, was attacked and burnt down by angry handloom weavers, an incident which is recorded by the Hammonds as a straight factory fire and not as a precursor of Luddism.

The difference is one of the skill, size, and organisation of the two groups; the Yorkshire croppers were a small, highly skilled body of 3-5,000 in all, who none the less had effective control of the vital finishing processes in the making of cloth, and were capable, when highly concentrated as in Leeds, of a high degree of organisation. The handloom weavers, by contrast, approached 200,000 in number, were a growing, unskilled body with easy access to their trade and widely scattered, and they lacked the organisation and cohesion of

their Yorkshire neighbours. And if they were otherwise engaged than in thinking about machinery in the years 1799-1812,
it was partly because there was no machinery which could
instantly and comprehensively wipe them out, the situation in
which the croppers found themselves. Cartwright's power-loom
was invented in 1785 and improved by him over the next few
years but it was too crude for general use. Radcliffe of Stockport invented a dressing-machine in 1803-4 which remedied
some of the existing defects by permitting the full preparation of the warp outside the loom, and the manufacture of
iron looms in 1803 was also a step forward. Yet in spite of
this a mere handful of innovators were using power-looms by
1812, and steam-weaving was making only a negligible impact
on the handloom weavers by this time. Though their plight
was unquestionably a serious one, arising from low wages
and unemployment during a period of inflation, power-looms
contributed insignificantly to this situation. Power-loom factories were evidently no great attraction to manufacturers and
investors on the evidence of Parkes' factory of 118 looms at
Westhoughton, which remained on the market for two years,
1806-8.[20]

It was estimated that in 1813 there were no more than 2,400
power-looms in Britain, while the number of handloom weavers was continuing to grow to over the 200,000 mark ten years
later. Only then did power-weaving begin to take over from
handloom weaving, and it is significant that a recent study
of the handloom weavers treats Lancashire Luddism as the
events of 1826, not those of 1812, and restricts comments
on 1812 Luddism to the Midlands area.[21]

Here then is some reason for questioning the importance
of the anti-machinery element in the Lancashire disturbances
of 1812. That the cotton operatives already had the experience
from spinning to see the impossibility and unwisdom of resistance to mechanisation, and that they were realistic enough
to know that they could not continue to mount large-scale
successful attacks on factories to prevent powered machinery
being applied in a major industry, are other points that have

been made to suggest that Lancashire Luddism was not a serious attempt to prevent the introduction of power-looms, even though they were singled out for destruction in 1812.

A case was, of course, made out against the machinery that was attacked in 1812, and it was the innovators who were the victims. Peter Marsland of Stockport had his life threatened and his factory fired because of his improvements to machinery for steam weaving, which, it was alleged, would throw thousands out of work. Radcliffe of Stockport was similarly chosen as 'the original projector of the obnoxious looms' believed to be causing present distress and 'the proprietor of a patent of a machine for dressing cotton warps to be made use of in such looms'. As such, he was, it was believed, thought a proper object for Luddite attention. Westhoughton mill, attacked on 24 April, contained 170-80 looms for steam-weaving, and the owners had themselves made considerable improvements in the machinery to enable them to produce high-quality goods; these improvements were allegedly a cause of distress. And Burtons, the proprietors of the Middleton factory attacked on 20 and 21 April, wove calicoes very largely by steam looms; these looms had halved the required man-power, and employees were said to have stated that it would be impossible for weavers to earn sufficient to support their families if factories weaving by steam were to become general. It was not simply resentment about the existing state of affairs but a fear of possible future developments which determined the weavers' conduct. One deponent testified to the belief among weavers that 45,000 of them were suffering from the steam looms as well as members of other trades and that an immediate international peace would make no difference to their plight unless the looms were put down.

Sometimes the argument was the vague one of the need 'to destroy all steam looms whereby it was thought trade would be bettered'. On other occasions a more idealistic note was struck when employers were asked to abandon their steam looms and dressing machines 'in justice to humanity'. Contemporaries in authority and historians in judgement have accepted that many genuinely believed that improved machinery was the cause of their plight, but they have not accepted that this was a correct belief.[22]

Both contemporaries and historians have been inclined to ask whether there was any point in introducing labour-saving machinery at a time of depression in the industry, and the abundance of cheap labour was undoubtedly a factor inhibiting the fuller conversion to powered weaving in later years, just as it was a factor in retarding the advent of powered stocking-frames in hosiery. The fact that labour-saving machinery was being extended during a period of unemployment has, in fact, suggested the interpretation that the depressed situation was being deliberately exploited by employers to weaken the position of the operatives even more by foisting the machines upon them to reduce their status at a time when they were least able to resist.[23]

It seems to be implied that the motivation behind the introduction of new machinery during the war period was not so much economic as social and political; that machinery was not being considered on its merits for the stimulus it would give to production but for the other effects it could produce, especially the depression of the workers into whose industries it was being introduced. The innovators are portrayed as a malicious and evil body of people rather than as a greedy, self-seeking group. It is suggested, for instance, that in hosiery 'the framework-knitters were beaten down to poverty during the wars' by a general process very similar to 'that by which the weavers were degraded'. The hosiers are said to have had two alternative ways of lowering wages to accomplish this, one being to reduce prices paid to workmen, the other the more indirect means of increasing frame-rents. As in hand-loom weaving, the least scrupulous employers were undermining conditions throughout the trade, and a further means of assisting their purpose was found in manufacturing 'cut-ups', a cheap technique of production which encouraged the influx of 'cheap and unskilled labour', turning framework-knitting into a debased, dishonourable trade. In this situation wages declined by an estimated one-third from their 1807 level.[24]

This is, in fact, a partial, even an 'ideologically mounted' view of the situation. The French wars, which the manufacturers of Nottingham had opposed at the very outset, produced problems that were common to both masters and men, and both the Luddites and the manufacturers were in their ways fellow-sufferers from its economic consequences. To stave off bankruptcy the manufacturers were, like the men, concerned to promote the general 'good of the trade' and they searched around for ways to do this. Wage-reductions, to lower production costs and stimulate business, were one attempted solution which a minority attempted, and it was over these reductions that Luddism began. Another possibility was the cheapening of articles by the introduction of lower-quality production, and this was attempted by the manufacture of 'cut-ups', but, far from having the result of cheapening labour, cut-up manufacture constituted the one growing-point of a very depressed industry and offered some of its best wages. It is interesting to note that a group of hosiers who supplied figures in 1812 in an attempt to show that they were still paying much the same wages in that year as they had over previous ones were heavily committed to cut-up manufacture. The problems which faced the hosiery trade during the Luddite period were common to both masters and men; a common crisis point was being reached by both sides and there was no more agreement amongst the masters about the solutions to be adopted than there was amongst the men about their best tactics for ameliorating their position. Many hosiers supported the men's efforts to secure parliamentary regulation of the trade in 1812, indicating that Luddism had failed to drive any great wedge between the two sides, and even Luddism had aims of which many hosiers would approve, whatever their repugnance to the methods being employed. The suggestion that Luddism was 'less . . . an agitation of workmen, than . . . an aspect of competition between the backward and the progressive . . . manufacturer, might be going too far, but the identical interests of the men and many of the masters preclude any judgement that Nottinghamshire Luddism was a class struggle between an oppressive employing class and an oppressed working class.[25]

Nor do the northern textile industries which experienced Luddism invite such an interpretation. Both the opposition provoked amongst fellow-manufacturers by the innovators in cloth-finishing prior to Yorkshire Luddism and the tiny minority role of the power-loom operators in Lancashire preclude any view of northern Luddism as a piece of class warfare. And where the innovators do attempt to introduce new machinery into their industries during the economic slump of the late war period (which very few do as far as Lancashire is concerned), it seems not unreasonable to interpret this, like the policies of some hosiers, as a response to the war conditions rather than as an attempt by unscrupulous men to exploit a situation for class advantage. Ideological commitment becomes a serious menace to historical writing if rational, intelligible actions which make sense according to the economic justification advanced to support them are to be explained only on the assumption that their perpetrators were malicious men, motivated by considerations that were more than selfish and positively wicked.[26]

Attempts to interpret personal motivation are always difficult. It could be, and was, argued that only by improving machinery could Britain remain ahead of her competitors for international trade, though the slowness with which the handloom weaver disappeared over the next decades suggests that the demands of trade were insufficient to create any great impulse towards technological advance in normal peace-time trading conditions. One commentator mused philosophically that 'it may be a question of speculative policy how far the extension of machinery be ultimately beneficial or prejudicial to the interests of a community'; at the same time he argued the expediency of having power-looms produce a given quantity, of equable quality, and at a reduced price, with the certainty of raw material being honestly applied, and condemned the folly of workmen for disregarding the principle that 'the in-

vention of machinery to abridge human labour is infallibly
followed by an increase of wages to artizans of every description'. In practice the advantages of the power-looms were
as much exaggerated as their supposed harmful consequences.
An impartial examination of the pros and cons of the case
has judged that, even after a fair number of large factories
had been established in England and Scotland, in 1815 'it
was still considered problematical whether the saving of labour
gained outweighed the expense involved in setting up and
maintaining the large establishment necessary for steam-weaving'. There were more than handloom weavers who lacked
enthusiasm for power-looms, though it is difficult to find any
evidence to support the workmen's view that the looms were
doing them any great harm.[27]

It would hardly be possible to maintain the irrelevance of
the machine issue as far as the Yorkshire cloth trade was concerned. It might be argued that the complete destruction of
all cloth-finishing machinery, gig-mills and shearing-frames
alike, would not have relieved the distress of the croppers in
the current economic situation, but this machinery was much
more than a dreamed-up threat to the croppers' status. As
far as the employers were concerned, the croppers were a
small number of men in relation to the total employed in
the industry, but with a totally disproportionate power, able to
restrict entry to their craft, maintain good wages for themselves, and frustrate repeated attempts to introduce labour-
saving machinery into the finishing side of the industry. The
gig-mill and the shearing-frame would be the manufacturers'
emancipation from the controls that the croppers exercised
over them; they would also do a quicker, cheaper, and more
efficient job than the cropper could, though he refused to accept
this last argument. And if the optimistic prognosis of the
1805 committee of enquiry was to be believed, machinery
could be introduced without impairing the comforts or lessen-
ing the number of the workmen involved, in spite of the alarms
which accompanied its introduction but which after a time
subsided. As the condemned Yorkshire Luddites were told

from the bench in January 1813, it was a gross delusion to foist upon them to suggest that the quantity of labour would be diminished by the new machinery being introduced. Yet delusion or not, this is what the croppers did feel, and not surprisingly.[28]

If contemporaries did not share modern suspicions about the motivation of the innovators, it was at least suggested by the *Leeds Mercury* that there was great difficulty involved in, and delicacy required on, the question of the expediency of using machinery in a department of the woollen industry where there were, unfortunately, numbers of men out of work. The writer refused to commit himself on the subject, and this in the middle-class *Mercury* of the manufacturing interests, for there was by no means a general welcome to the gig-mill and the shearing-frame among the employing class, whatever indignities they had suffered at the hands of the croppers. When William Cartwright began in 1809 to finish cloth by machinery at his water-powered Rawfolds mill, near Liversedge, he not only created resentment among workmen in the area but also alarm among smaller employers who were continuing to employ traditional methods and who were gradually forced to close down in the face of this competition. A similar division inside the manufacturers was reported from Leeds between those who were attempting to become workers of the gigs and frames and those who were still organising their business traditionally, and this division at the employer level produced several charges of collusion between Luddites and renegade employers. These developments must be seen, too, against the whole rise of the factory system in cloth manufacture, a development deplored by non-participating manufacturers as well as workmen, for it was the factory-owner who was most active in promoting the introduction of the gigs and shearing-frames. Herbert Heaton, the woollen industry's most distinguished historian, argued that, along with the workmen, the small independent clothiers were fighting for their very existence in resisting labour-saving machinery and trying to stop the flow to the factory. The cost of installing new machinery meant

that only the large operators would be able to take advantage
of improvements in mechanisation, and so the small men
fought to preserve and revive the Act of 1555 which prohibited
gig-mills and forbade the congregating of machinery into one
place. They supported the proposed Bill of 1795 'for restoring
and preserving entire the late system of carrying on the cloth
manufacturing' and ten years later petitioned for a Bill to
limit looms, suppress gigs and enforce apprenticeship rules.

But whatever the feeling of the master clothier or cloth
merchant, it was the cropper who really felt the pinch when
the threat of mechanisation arose. It was all very well for
a judge to deliver homilies on fallacious arguments concerning the diminished quantity of labour a mechanised industry
could employ, but what the new machines could and did do
was, in the course of a small number of years, to eliminate
the need for a particular skill and thereby eliminate a particular occupation that had previously been relatively well
paid, carrying a wage of up to thirty shillings (£1.50) a week in
the early part of the century. The croppers had a strong
vested interest in preserving the status quo and cannot be
blamed for any lack of historical perspective or inability to
foresee long-term development. We cannot wish that they
had succeeded in halting technological advance, yet they cannot be blamed for wanting to do so.[29]

It is now possible to draw together some of the threads
and to look at Luddism in the broad context of the Industrial Revolution. One suggestion has been that Luddism
represents the crisis point for the new economic principles
and moral values of laissez-faire when they triumph over
both the traditional paternalism of the state and the rival
moral economy that the working classes are putting forward
through Luddism. Against this it must be said that in the
hosiery trade capitalism had triumphed long before 1811. The
high cost of both machines and materials determined that the
industry should be organised on a capitalist basis from the
start, and the independent frame-owner had joined the minority ranks before 1775.

Also, the movement of the industry from London to the provinces had early ensured that the paternalist charter of Charles II should cease to regulate the trade, and the apparent revival of the old Framework-Knitters' Company for a brief spell in 1805-9 should not be allowed to obscure its decades of insignificance before this time. 1811 is not a meaningful date in the abrogation of paternalist legislation as far as hosiery was concerned; the legislation had lapsed into disregard long before that time. In the woollen-cloth trade the paternalist provisions abandoned by Parliament in 1806 and 1809 concerned not only workmen's rights to be protected against the introduction of labour-saving machinery and the maintenance of proper apprenticeship, but also a whole series of petty technical restrictions on the manufacturer in the making of cloth, which 'worse than insane measures' were believed to have 'cost the clothier more by limiting his operations in the field of industry than any damage done by the Luddites'. And on the point at issue in 1812, the gig-mills and shearing-frames, the areas most actively involved in machine-breaking were those where mechanisation had been furthest extended, from as early as the 1780s. The date 1812 seems more meaningful in the context of war and trade depression than in terms of the history of technological advance. Similarly, the year seems of little significance outside this context in Lancashire, in view of the quarter of a century's relative absence of protest against the power-looms which were the object of Luddite hostility in 1812. The demand for and refusal of a legal minimum wage, the principal workers' demand for limiting unfettered capitalism, appear to have had no place in Luddite agitation of 1812, when machinery was the issue at stake.[30]

It also seems unsatisfactory to find the crisis point for economic individualism in an age of industrial revolution arising out of these particular examples. It is true that in each case there is present the element of the 'big man', the 'cut-up' manufacturer, the factory owner finishing cloth by machinery, and the cotton-mill owner weaving by power, against the 'little' man who represents the traditional way of doing things;

but it is only in the tiny cropping-trade that we see the classic Industrial Revolution pattern and dilemma in existence. The depressed stocking-knitters were not the victims of the Industrial Revolution; their problem was that it was passing them by, that their industry was becoming obsolete in technology through the failure to apply steam power to the stocking-frame, and, obsolete in organisation through the failure to move away from the domestic system to a factory unit of production; these failures were not rectified until the second half of the nineteenth century. The Nottinghamshire Luddites were the victims of industrial decay; their need was more not less machinery, and they were hardly torch-bearers for the new industrial proletariat which was being created by the Industrial Revolution. Nor were the handloom weavers fighting a key battle against the forces of industrialisation in 1812; the machinery they opposed came in slowly over half a century, during the first half of which they made little protest and during the second part of which they grew in number simultaneously with the increase in power-loom weaving. Again, the handloom weavers of 1812 were neither the new industrial proletariat nor the obvious and immediate victims of the Industrial Revolution. For this latter role we must turn to the few thousand croppers whose craft was being eliminated and who would have to find what alternative employment they could; in this body of men can be seen the victims of the Industrial Revolution. But if generalisations are being sought about the working-class experience in the age of industrial revolution they must be sought amongst larger groups than this. And if generalisations are being sought about Luddism they must take into account the fact that in only one area was machine-breaking an attempt to prevent industrial change by technological advance, that in the Midlands the Luddites had no prospect of industrial change through technological advance, and that in Lancashire Luddism was of only marginal and doubtful relevance to the issue.[31]

A few other questions remain to be posed about the cause of Luddism, not the least of which is why men should choose to break machines as the specific response to the discontent and distress that they experienced. It might seem obvious that discontent with shearing-frames, gig-mills, 'cut-up' frames and steam-looms should result in attacks upon these particular machines, but the Luddites, in choosing to break machines, were not simply lashing out blindly against the object of their hatred. If these particular machines could have been prevented or eliminated by some other means, by agreement, for instance, between workmen and employers, there would have been no need to resort to the physical violence and illegal enterprises of Luddism. The 'solicitor to General Ludd' wrote to inform the Huddersfield magistrate, Joseph Radcliffe, that as the cloth-dressers of the area had spent £7,000 in petitioning the government to uphold legislation against shearing-frames and gigs, and all to no purpose, they were now trying another method. From Lancashire, a Bolton deponent expressed an identical sentiment; the Home Secretary had been approached, the government had given them no satisfaction, and so it became necessary to take the means into their own hands. Luddism was a last resort when other techniques had been tried and had proved useless; trade-union negotiation had achieved nothing for any of the workers involved, save the croppers of Leeds in their special position; more efficient, orthodox industrial action through trade-union organisation was both illegal and very difficult to achieve in scattered, domestic industries of low-paid workers, and political power was either beyond their means as unenfranchised workers or, in the case of the Nottingham stockingers who were enfranchised if duly apprenticed, beyond their concept.

In Nottinghamshire the framework-knitters, persuaded to make one further attempt in 1812 to secure parliamentary redress of grievance, saw their efforts collapse and were thereby encouraged to look again towards machine-breaking as a possible solution to their problems. The Nottingham framework-knitters could not even cling to the belief that possession of votes allowed them to make themselves heard and forced people to listen to them, for they constituted half the Notting-

ham electorate anyway and little good it had done them, in
part because it had not occurred to them at this time to use
their political power as voters to achieve the industrial aims
which they pursued as workers. The power that could be
obviously and immediately wielded by the workman was the
power to damage or destroy the property of his employer,
which was either within the workman's own keeping or at
least within his reach.[32]

An interesting attempt has been made to look at the political
and economic geography of Luddism. It has been suggested
that in urban centres, where entire industries were partially
paralysed by the consequences of war and employers were
themselves active in demonstrating and petitioning against
the government and its Orders in Council, the discontent of
the working classes assumed more constitutional forms, that
the problems of order were less where employers were themselves hostile to the administration. This attractive thesis is,
unfortunately, undermined by an included example and a
highly relevant omission. The example of Manchester, which
had all the ingredients of the 1812 disturbances, food riots,
political riots, and anti-machinery demonstrations, seems
hardly appropriate to illustrate working-class constitutional
protest. Nor would the town of Nottingham have been so,
where an entire industry was partially paralysed and manufacturers had denounced government folly from the very
beginning of the wars in 1793; there was no provincial centre
more committed to attacks on government and administration
than Nottingham, yet this town was also the principal seat of
Luddism in the entire country.[33]

Another factor that prompted contemporary discussion was
the spread of Luddism once the outbreak had begun, and here
any mildly sympathetic reporting of Luddism in the press was
held to be an encouragement to the work of the machine-
breakers. In Nottingham, the radical *Review* attempted to
explain the grievances of the workmen as well as to censure
their conduct, and this brought storms of protest from the
Journal, which portrayed their rival's writers as fellow-travel-

lers with the machine-breakers. The independent line taken by
the *Review* editor and owner and his less than deferential attitude towards authority eventually led to his being sent to
Northampton jail for printing a satirical letter, allegedly from
a British soldier serving in America, who claimed to be per-
forming much more wicked deeds serving his country as a
hero than he had ever performed back home as a criminal
Luddite a couple of years earlier. And a similar situation
existed in Leeds, where the ultra-Tory *Leeds Intelligencer*
censured the liberal *Mercury* for supposedly encouraging the
trouble-makers with its over-sympathetic treatment of the issue
of machine-breaking, though the *Mercury* had always un-
equivocally condemned the machine-breakers and their
methods.[34]

It must remain a matter for speculation to what extent
machine-breaking in the north of England occurred in simple
imitation of the activities of the Nottinghamshire Luddites.
Without at this stage a prejudgement of the extent of the
connections between the different disturbed parts of the
country, it can be said that the Nottinghamshire example was
held to be dangerous and harmful to the prospects of peace
elsewhere. Magistrate Fletcher of Bolton expressed his concern on 21 January 1812 at the dangerous example that
Nottingham had set to a manufacturing area such as his own.
When the Yorkshire Luddites were brought to trial, the
counsel for the prosecution gave his account of the reactions
of the indicted men to the transactions at Nottingham, news
'which these men were unfortunately in the habit of reading
in the newspapers', and men were later described as having
acted 'in imitation of the frame-breakers at Nottingham'. So
convinced was the *Leeds Intelligencer* on this point that it
demanded the punishment of those papers which had published the Nottingham news.[35]

One last point, which again touches on a bigger theme,
still to be discussed, is the role of government provocation and
instigation in the causation of Luddism. The tale told by
Gravener Henson to Place has already been mentioned, and

E

this interpretation was not unique. At least one historian has suggested that workmen's grievances against machinery were made use of by designing persons to enable the government to crush the new political life rising into being, which is a slightly more moderate view. So, too, is the opinion that spies were actively at work amongst the discontented, 'fanning the disaffection of the operatives in order to betray them'. Spies there undoubtedly were, and their role will be examined later, but it is probably true to say that they were not a prime cause of Luddism but rather came into play once Luddism was launched, though it does seem certain that one at least of the Luddite coups in Lancashire, the Westhoughton job, was conceived by spies long before the attack was actually accomplished.[36]

In summary it can be said that all the workmen involved in Luddism had specific grievances in their own industrial context which other forms of action had failed to remove, that these particular grievances were most consciously felt in the intensely depressed situation of 1811-12 when a commercial crisis and bad harvests combined to produce famine prices and wages at starvation level, and that machine-breaking, more or less closely identified with the real purpose of the Luddites, suggested itself as the last viable way of making their protest felt. Once begun, Luddism was then extended and reshaped by a host of new factors which developed, such as the commercialism of the Nottinghamshire Luddite, the diverted attention of the Yorkshire Luddite towards arms thefts and robbery in general, and the confusion created by spies in the Lancashire scene.

1 Thompson, E. P. *The Making* . . . . p 543
2 *Leeds Intelligencer*, 20 January 1812; HO 42/123, Maitland to HO, 4 May 1812; HO 42/120, Lloyd to HO, 26 February 1812; HO 42/129, Higgins to HO, 2 November 1812
3 HO 42/117, Newcastle to HO, 16 December 1811; HO 40/1, 'Ned Ludd' to Mr Smith, undated; *Leeds Intelligencer*, 6 July 1812; HO 42/121, Haines to HO, 22 March 1812; Nottingham

Borough Records, M429, F26; *Leeds Mercury*, 7 December 1811

4 British Museum Additional MSS 27809, Place's account of the years 1815 onwards p 18

5 Cited by Bythell, D. *The Handloom Weavers* p 102; See HO 42/117; HO 40/1, Fletcher to HO, 6 May 1812; HO 42/123, Maitland to HO, 6 May 1812

6 Fitzwilliam MSS, eg 46/15, 46/47; *Leeds Mercury*, 1 August 1812; HO 42/127, Maitland to HO, 12 September 1812; HO 42/121, Clay to HO, 23 March 1812; HO 42/123, Wigfull to HO, 17 May 1812; Peel, F. *The Risings of the Luddites* (1880) pp 6-8

7 *Nottingham Review*, 8, 22 May 1812; Felkin, W. *History of the Machine Wrought Hosiery and Lace Manufacturers* (1867) p 239. Story of William Felkin III by himself

8 TS (Treasury Solicitors' papers) 11/980, 3580

9 Fitzwilliam MSS, 45/143, 47/45, 47/49; Crump, W. *The Leeds Woollen Industry* (1931) p 45; eg HO 40/2, Chesterton to HO, 9 January 1813

10 HO 42/124, Précis of General Maitland's communication from Manchester, 19 June 1812; HO 42/120, I. Kayer to HO, 11 February, 1812; HO 40/1, Fletcher to HO, 11 April 1812; Manchester Central Reference Library, Misc 213/3, Mosley 3

11 HO 42/130, 21 December 1812; HO 40/2, Macdougal to HO, 6 November 1812

12 First Report of Select Committee on Framework-Knitters' Petitions, 1812, 11, pp 10-11; Wells, F. A. *The British Hosiery Trade* (1935) p 99; Report of Select Committee on Laws affecting Export of Machinery, 1841, VII, Appendix 3, p 233; Felkin, W. *History of the Machine Wrought Hosiery* . . . . 1867) p 230

13 *Leeds Mercury*, 7 December 1811

14 Bythell, D. *The Handloom Weavers* p 199

15 HO 42/117, Newcastle to HO, 16 November 1811; Parliamentary Debates, Vol 57, 967, 26 February 812; *Nottingham Review*, 6 December 1811

16 HO 42/119, Oates, Wood and Smithson to HO, 22 January 1812; Radcliffe MSS 126/27.

17 eg HO 42/120, Lloyd to HO, 11 February 1812

18 Crump, W. B. and Ghorbal, G. *History of the Huddersfield Woollen Industry* (1935) Ch X; *Leeds Mercury*, 25 January 1812

19 Crump, W. B. and Ghorbal, G. *History of the Huddersfield*

Woollen Industry Ch X; *Leeds Intelligencer*, 4 May, 13 April 1812; Peel, F. *Spen Valley Past and Present* (1893) p 238; *Historical Account of the Luddites* (1862) p 9

20 *Manchester Commercial Advertiser*, 24 March 1812; Hammond, J. L. & B. *The Skilled Labourer* (1919) pp 69-89; Bythell, D. *The Handloom Weavers* pp 74-82

21 Ibid pp 57, 193, 197-204

22 HO 42/122, G. Hadfield to HO, 20 April 1812; HO 40/1, Lloyd to HO, 21 March 1812; TS 11/980, 3582; TS 11/980, 3580; HO 40/1, unsigned, undated deposition before Charles Prescot; Ibid, statement of H. Yarwood, 22 June 1812

23 eg *Leeds Mercury*, 25 January 1812; Thompson, E. P. *The Making* . . . . pp 529-30

24 Ibid pp 530, 533, 543

25 Second Report of Select Committee on Framework-Knitters' Petitions, 1812, 11, pp 65-100; Hobsbawm, E. J. *The Machine Breakers*

26 Peel, F. *Spen Valley Past and Present* p 238; Crump, W. B. and Ghorbal, G. *History of the Huddersfield Woollen Industry* (1935) pp 90-1

27 'Bishop Blaze's address to "The Misguided Men who destroy Machinery" '; *Manchester Commercial Advertiser*, 21 April 1812; Tupling, G. H. *The Economic History of Rossendale* (1927) pp 210-11

28 Crump, W. B. and Ghorbal, G. *History of the Huddersfield Woollen Industry* p 95; *Leeds Mercury*, 9 January 1813

29 *Leeds Mercury*, 25 January 1812; Peel, F. *Spen Valley Past and Present* p 238; HO 42/122, Ikin to HO, 15 April 1812; Heaton, H. *The Yorkshire Woollen and Worsted Industries* (1965 edit) p 321

30 Thompson, E. P. *The Making* . . . . p 543; Wells, F. A. *The British Hosiery Trade* (1935) p 69; Chambers, J. D. 'The Worshipful Company of Framework-knitters, 1657-1778', *Economica*, 1929; *Historical Account* p IV

31 Chambers, J. D. 'Victorian Nottingham', *Transactions of the Thoroton Society*, 1959; *The Vale of Trent 1670-1800*, p 60

32 Radcliffe MSS 126/27; HO 42/128, deposition of Oliver Nicholson

33 Thompson, E. P. *The Making* . . . . p 564

34 Sutton, J. F. *Nottingham Date Book* pp 316-18; *Nottingham Review*, 1 September 1815; *Leeds Intelligencer*, 20 July 1812

35 HO 42/119, Fletcher to HO, 21 January 1812; *Leeds Mercury*, 9 January 1813; *Leeds Intelligencer*, 11 January 1813

36 Axon, W. E. A. *Echoes of Old Lancashire* (1899) p 171;
    Watts, J. *The Facts of the Cotton Famine* (1866) p 28; HO
    40/1, Fletcher to HO, 6 April 1812

Chapter Three

THE AIMS OF
THE LUDDITES

IT COULD BE argued that to distinguish between the aims of
the Luddites and the causes of Luddism is to introduce a
distinction that does not properly exist, for the Luddites clearly
sought to eliminate or solve those problems which brought
them into existence. On the other hand, Luddism was not a
static movement but a developing and evolving one, which
soon began to depart from the causes which had first given
it its being. And so it is necessary to look at the aims of the
Luddites as their movement developed, as well as to restate
their initial basic programme of industrial aims.

The first act of machine-breaking in Nottinghamshire
occurred after a lengthy attempt by a group of hosiery firms
to use such organisation as their workmen possessed to persuade the stockingers not to accept work from their trade
rivals at a reduced price, a not uncommon shifting of the
responsibility for price-maintenance on to the shoulders of the
workmen themselves. The attempt broke down and the five
firms, including Thomas Brocksopp & Company, introduced a
cut in their own wages, protesting their reluctance to do this
but justifying it on the ground of their inability otherwise to
compete with their undercutting rivals. They laid particular
blame on the workers of privately-owned frames who were
allegedly accepting cheap work, something they were freer
to do than the majority whose frames were owned by the
hosier for whom they worked. Unhappily for this group of

hosiers, the majority of the remaining firms chose to dissociate themselves from the stand and announced their intention to abide by list prices. The five were then placed in the position of seeming to be exploiting the war situation to bring down wages; perhaps it would be fairer to say that some manufacturers were hoping to combat the current trade depression by reducing production costs and thereby stimulating trade. At all events, the move precipitated the outbreak of machine-breaking in Arnold, just to the north of Nottingham, on 11 March 1812 and it was on the question of wage reductions that it arose.[1]

Much of the current debate was about 'the unprincipled oppression of an avaricious few' on one side and poor workmen on the other, pitied by the Duke of Newcastle for having been badly treated by their employers. The Rev J. T. Becher, a county magistrate of Southwell, spoke of the 'honour and humanity' of the majority of employers as opposed to the undercutting tactics of others, with their profits 'oppressively extorted from the starving necessities of the poor', and Lord Middleton also expressed the view that but for the conduct of the hosiers there would have been no Luddism. There seems unanimity amongst contemporary authorities, including William Felkin, who participated in the events of these times and later wrote their history, that Luddism arose out of wage reductions. This was what George Coldham, the town clerk at Nottingham, informed the Home Secretary and this is what the London police officers, Conant and Baker, concluded when they investigated the developments there; and so it is not surprising that some have continued to believe that the first and only real object of the Luddites was to preserve wage rates.[2]

But this is too simple a view, and it disregards the fact that Luddism, once launched, became a most complicated phenomenon and that motives and purposes proliferated as machine-breaking was extended. Undoubtedly the theme of preserving wages remained; it can be clearly seen in the machine-breaking of the spring of 1814 and in the greatest of all Midland Luddite coups, the attack on the Loughborough lace factory of John

Heathcoat in June 1816, which arose because of the prices
being paid by Heathcoat. But this theme was supplemented by
others. Frames were broken because they were being operated
by 'colts' or unapprenticed workers, a threat to the position of
the properly-trained man and a hazard to production stand-
ards; they were broken because their owners were accused of
payments in truck or of imposing other intolerable abatements
upon the men; most of all, they were broken because they were
'wide' ones on which 'cut-up' hosiery was manufactured, that
is articles which were cut and stitched into shape from broad
pieces of knitwear, without proper selvages and without the
capacity to survive washing and reasonable wear. Such articles
were, allegedly, throwing the whole trade into disrepute and
undermining the position of the fully-fashioned, traditionally-
manufactured product.

In other words, the whole range of stockingers' grievances,
which can be seen from the 1812 attempt to secure parliamentary regulation of the trade, became part of the Luddite programme once it was launched, especially the grievance
about 'cut-up' manufacture; it was the 'cut-up' frame that was
selected by the Luddite for particular treatment, though there
is some reason to suppose that this was a piece of rationalisa-
tion rather than the basic grievance, which was wages. Brocksopp had himself declared against cut-ups, but once Luddism
was launched the frame-breakers appear to have looked
around for other possible causes of their present misery and
to have extended their campaign beyond the initial purpose
of attempting to preserve wage rates. Some contemporaries
even felt that Luddism in Nottinghamshire was building up
into something of an industry, with jobs being found to keep
the machine-breakers at work, and the money which appears
to have changed hands over the breaking episodes suggests
strongly that a vested interest was created in the perpetration
of frame-breaking, which acquired a commercialism not in
evidence elsewhere.[3]

The industrial programme of the Yorkshire Luddites is
clear enough in that Yorkshire Luddism was an attempt to

achieve by other means aims which the men had long been pursuing by more orthodox trade-union organisation, namely the defeat of the manufacturers' efforts to introduce shearing-frames and gig-mills, though, in the case of the latter, their use was sufficiently established by 1812 outside Leeds to suggest that only in that town was there any real hope of checking their introduction. It would not be unreasonable to see behind the croppers' campaign against the shearing-frame and gig-mill a desire to reimpose the whole of the protective legislation suspended and repealed in 1806 and 1809 by which, amongst other things, their ability to control entry to their craft had been undermined, but it might be over-imaginative to see Yorkshire Luddism as a revolt against the factory system as such. As far as can be shown, in 1812 the factory-owners were offensive because they pioneered the introduction of powered, labour-saving machinery rather than because they were factory-owners.[4]

To argue the contrary it becomes necessary to analyse the 'unconscious motives' of the croppers, an exercise in psychoanalysis for which the historian is not particularly well equipped, and one which tempts him to ascribe motivation and purpose to Luddism on the basis of what it should have been rather than what it was. The over-romanticised Luddites then emerge as champions of all the best working-class causes of the future, a legal minimum wage, opposition to sweated labour, compensation for redundancy, trade unionism, and the ten-hour movement, rather than as machine-breakers, which is like arguing that the Luddites were a literate, humorous, and politically experienced body of men because Gravener Henson and a few Nottingham colleagues revealed these qualities when involved in a parliamentary petition which had nothing to do with Luddism.[5]

As far as the Luddism of Lancashire is concerned, it has already been suggested that the precise industrial aims of the workmen are difficult to determine. Attacks on steam-looms developed out of a background of attempts to secure a minimum wage and parliamentary regulation of the trade. They were not employed, as in Nottinghamshire, in an attempt to hold particular employers to particular prices; nor does it seem realistic to suppose that they were employed, as in Yorkshire, in a serious attempt to stop mechanisation; that they had no prospects of doing this and had previously shown little inclination to do it where steam-loom weaving was concerned both suggest that the anti-machinery movement in Lancashire was more a general protest movement against conditions as a whole than one designed to secure precise industrial ends. This lack of definition in the purpose of the Lancashire Luddites left them more prone to the charges and accusations of contemporaries about a supposed political purpose than did the relatively clear aims of their brethren across the Pennines and in Nottinghamshire.

The perplexing problem that every investigator of the Luddites has had to face is that of trying to determine whether their aims were purely or mainly industrial and whether the apparent industrial aims were a cover for a more serious political ambition.

Joseph Radcliffe was informed that as soon as the obnoxious machinery was stopped or destroyed the general and his army would disband and return to their employment like other loyal subjects; on the other hand, the informer Yarwood, recounting his days as a trade unionist and Luddite, recalled the moment when he 'conceived that something further than the destruction of the steam-looms or machinery was intended'. Nor was Yarwood, he regretted to say, able to reveal 'the ultimate object of the secret Committee' for he did not know it. The undisclosed purpose of the secret agency is a theme which runs through contemporary observations on Luddism. There is 'some hidden mystery in it not yet ready for development' wrote the *Leeds Intelligencer*; 'there is a dark, subtle and invisible agency at work, seducing the ignorant and the inexperienced. The croppers and the stocking weavers are but the deluded instruments of this agency'. Similarly J. Lloyd wrote from Stockport of having 'reason to fear that the secret Engines are at work and plots un-

connected with the destruction of machinery further than that
may serve to increase general distress'. Luddism, wrote another, was being promoted 'by some secret instigators of
rebellion from other parts of England'. Some with these suspicions would hazard a guess at the identity of these secret
agencies; others just felt that there was more to Luddism than
machine-breaking and that what they were witnessing was not
the last or even the worst instalment of the drama. Joseph
Radcliffe feared that the present spirit would not end with
the destruction of new inventions to expedite manufacture,
and the House of Commons Committee of Secrecy was speaking for many when it admitted its inability to say what the
ultimate object of the men was; at the same time it strongly
suggested its conviction that there was an ultimate unrevealed
object beyond the immediate, disclosed one.[6]

The problem was in part, and this was recognised, that
Luddism was all the time changing, that men started out with
one idea, that something happened and one thing led to another; Luddism acquired a momentum of its own and it was
genuinely difficult to see its ultimate outcome. If the obnoxious
machinery were allowed to remain in use, wrote one of
Radcliffe's correspondents, the dispute over machinery would
probably terminate in civil war. This was a particularly
pessimistic forecast, but the difficulties involved in setting a
limit to aims and conduct, once an illegal enterprise such as
Luddism had been launched, were clearly seen. Baron Thompson's address at the York Assizes contained a moderate enough
account of the progressive build-up of Luddism when he suggested that from the destruction of machines men moved
readily enough to attacks upon buildings: this involved large
bodies of men, and when such numbers came together for
illegal purposes they rapidly moved from one cause to the
next. The destruction of buildings led to the stealing of fire-
arms for carrying out the attacks, and the stealing of arms
led to indiscriminate theft of every kind of property.

The evolution of Yorkshire Luddism does in fact illustrate
this theme particularly well. At a certain point in time it

became necessary for the croppers either to rest contented with the small, successful jobs they had accomplished or to strike a really big blow against one of their main opponents who had held out against their campaign and provoked them by his determination and resolution. They chose to press on and mount a full-scale attack upon the Rawfolds Mill of William Cartwright, which, if successful, would constitute a major triumph for the anti-machinery campaign and consolidate the prestige and standing of the Luddites. The attack was a failure and two Luddites were killed. According to General Grey the Rawfolds affair had the effect of frightening the Luddites and making them very cautious about proceeding to any further acts of violence, but a contrary view was more widely held. Grey had himself previously learned that 'Vengeance for the blood of the Innocent' was written on every door after the death of the two men, and there seems little doubt that the successful assassination of William Horsfall of Marsden and the abortive attempts on the lives of Cartwright, Joseph Radcliffe and Colonel Campbell were direct consequences of the deaths of the two Luddites. Finding themselves unable to destroy large establishments by force, wrote the Huddersfield Secret Committee, opposed to the Luddites, the depredators have changed their plan and now hope to accomplish their purpose by assassination.

It was the use of soldiers against them and the shooting of two of their colleagues that caused the Yorkshire Luddites to take serious steps to provide themselves with arms, by theft if necessary, and the situation which developed in consequence seemed to the deputy-lieutenant of the West Riding, Sir Francis Wood, to bear a strong resemblance to that in Ireland in 1797-8, with their outrages leading the Luddites along a direct route to open insurrection. And this had started from a decision to break offensive industrial machinery. Wood's view, which he contradicted on other occasions, has of late been supported and developed, and it has been suggested that after Rawfolds the Luddites shifted their emphasis to 'general insurrectionary preparations' based on a 'serious conspiratorial organisation' which was coming into existence. Its work is illustrated by a description of an arms raid upon the village of Clifton, between Cleckheaton and Brighouse, but there is not much in this to suggest revolutionary plans, especially when it is conceded that housebreakers, whom the authorities were by this time regarding as the most serious problem they had to face, were making a sizeable contribution to the disorder that remained.[7]

It was further suggested in describing the evolving nature of Luddism that people were drawn into it and that its character changed once it was an established phenomenon, General Maitland felt that in Lancashire many people were sucked into a progressing movement for whatever motives of sympathy or wish for excitement, but, finding themselves at the mercy of the mischievous intrigues of the individuals who drew them in, soon became anxious to make their escape. In Nottinghamshire there seems to have been a reverse process of people attaching themselves to the movement to exploit it for their own particular purposes and turning it towards self-aggrandisement and away from the social purposes which it had in its initial stages. Again, this view of Lancashire Luddism has been carried much further and it has been suggested that after Westhoughton and Middleton attacks upon power-looms came to an end, to be replaced by 'more serious insurrectionary preparations' which are illustrated in a letter from J. Lloyd of Stockport to the Home Secretary in mid-June, in which he alleged that bodies of upwards of a hundred men had been entering houses night after night in search of arms. This seems a gross exaggeration; such a force would have been most unwieldy and it would have involved a quite unnecessary waste of manpower to attack with that number anything short of a stately home. Also, it seems highly unwise to base a judgement on Lloyd's unique statement; local press accounts, which indicate that Lancashire experienced a similar round of arms thefts and general robberies to that in Yorkshire, contain no suggestion of the sort of scale and frequency described by Lloyd, the supreme example of a petty official

determined to carve a career out of the suppression of Luddism.[8]

The central fear of the opponents of the Luddites was that
armed insurrection or rebellion was being planned, and it is
this belief, real or alleged, that must now be examined. Two
injunctions should be borne in mind: it is important to avoid
jumping to the conclusions that because spies and informers
emphasised the most extreme features of a movement these
features were necessarily non-existent, and that because there
was no middle-class involvement in Luddism there was necessarily no political content; that a working-class movement was
incapable on its own of planning such a movement or organising its own revolution should not be assumed. It is necessary
to know what people thought and said, what they meant by the
terminology they employed, and on what sort of evidence
they reached their opinions.[9]

It is not difficult to find examples of people who wrote to
inform the Home Secretary, or his local representative, of their
belief that the Luddites were planning a revolution; there was
the Stockport correspondent of 20 April who said that the
Luddites had no other object than rebellion against the government, or the Cheadle man who wrote on 27 April that Luddism was not a question of low wages or want of work but a
'complete revolutionary system now pervading the whole part
of this Country'. It was on the basis of letters like this that the
government offered the opinion, later abandoned, that there
was a 'deep laid system' for overthrowing the government of
the country, especially when the letters became somewhat more
specific, offering not so much evidence of but confidence in
the belief that an actual rising of the Luddites was planned
and that it would occur on a particular day. Francis Raynes,
a captain in the Stirlingshire Militia, and heavily involved in
tracking down Luddites, later put on record his earlier belief
that the Luddites might attempt to rise in a body. The naming
of a date came particularly from Lancashire sources. Ralph
Wright of Flixton informed the Home Secretary on 19 April
that the rising of the people had been fixed for 1 May; this was

a notion popularly believed, but a few days later an Oldham correspondent named 4 May as the day chosen for the general rising. On 26 April R. A. Fletcher of Bolton, one of the Home Secretary's most regular correspondents, confirmed that there was no doubt about the early attempt to be made at insurrection throughout the manufacturing areas and even in the capital itself.

Most of the letters on the basis of which the Home Secretary attempted to assess the situation were from local officials such as Fletcher, who were concerned to get what information they could by whatever means they could and whose judgement was simply wrong when they attempted to forecast the outcome of the activities around them. Some other letters were clearly from a lunatic fringe of people whose scare stories were not based on any real attempt to assess their local situation but were the products of vivid or disturbed imagination. Such was the wild letter from York of 15 July which intimated that it would soon be too late to stop the rebellion, that Burdett and Whitbread were providing great encouragement to the Luddites through their speeches, that most of the men in York Castle were about to escape, and that the writer found himself surrounded by Luddites, a particularly unlikely event in York and suggesting that he was something of a neurotic. A similar letter came from Oldham on 22 May in which the writer talked of the village of Royton where everyone, save for five or six inhabitants, was a 'most determined and revolutionary Jacobin'. Another letter which showed a totally unrealistic assessment of the local situation came from Sheffield in mid-May; the writer described, accurately enough, the local desperation arising from distress, but then talked of 'many thousands of horrid wretches desirous of taking advantage' of the present situation to promote riot, insurrection, and revolution. Yet Sheffield had, only a few weeks previously, provided an outstanding example of a large food riot in which the local populace had stormed the arsenal of the local militia, not to capture the weapons therein and so arm themselves for revolutionary action, but to destroy the weapons, as an angry, desperate protest crowd might do.[10]

Not all the Home Secretary's correspondence suggested to
him that the country was on the threshold of a revolution, and
not all contemporaries believed that Luddism had anything
to do with politics. The most detailed and reasoned assess-
ments of the disturbed areas which the Home Office received
came from General Maitland, whose military role was extended
through 1812 to the point where he became supreme com-
mander of the effort to put down the Luddites. Maitland's
almost daily reports to the Home Secretary show a conscien-
tious, balanced man at work, listening to all the rumours and
conflicting accounts that local magistrates, informers and well-
wishers are able to produce for him, attempting to reconcile
them with each other, and trying to sift the worthwhile from
the spurious.

On his arrival in the disturbed part of Lancashire at the
beginning of May, when he was being deluged with local
opinion, he believed that the real cause of all the trouble was
'a combination to overcome all legal authority', but even at
this point he felt that the whole business had been 'over-
thought and exaggerated'; nor did he believe that a rising of
the people was seriously intended or that there was any great
danger to be feared at that time, and this was in the very heat
of the period that had been popularly predicted as the occasion for the insurrection. And the longer Maitland remained
in the area, the more he learned of the situation and the more
he saw of the way it was being handled by the local authorities,
the more inclined he was to believe that they were frightening
themselves by their inefficiency and incompetence, and the
more sceptical he became about the revolution gossip he
picked up. By 23 May he was reporting that if there were any
people concerned with revolutionary objectives their numbers
were small and their plans and objectives crude and indigested,
and that mischief was unlikely to increase to any extent. By
mid-June he could still find no evidence of revolutionary intention other than what could be seen in the open acts of
violence, and these were hardly indicative of a plan. And when

he moved over to Yorkshire shortly afterwards he was alarmed
at the terror provoked by the robberies but believed that the
mischievous spirit abroad had no head.

According to the *Leeds Mercury,* the disturbances were unconnected with political men and political parties, and it went
on to suggest that there had never been a combination of this
extent in Britain or elsewhere which had been so entirely free
from all political objectives and so entirely lacking in political
character. The same view was taken by the *Nottingham Review.*
Some were convinced that the political charge was a false one;
others were simply sceptical, in view of the apparent absence of
evidence to support the charges against the Luddites. Richard
Walker, for instance, wrote from Huddersfield on 9 July to
say that a number of neighbouring gentlemen were strongly
apprehensive of great political danger but were unable to give
a very convincing reason for their fear; while Joseph Radcliffe
himself admitted to having seen no strong evidence suggesting
a concerted political design. If these men were relying less on
evidence and more on what they felt to be their natural instinct
to sense political sedition, their instinct on this occasion played
them false, for there is little more evidence now to suggest the
correctness of their view, beyond that which they themselves
possessed.[11]

It is important that such evidence as does exist for the
supposed Luddite insurrection plan should be examined in
some detail, for it is this, not the mistaken opinions of observers, which can throw light on the degree of large-scale planning within the movement. Also, much of the actual evidence
leads to the very fringes of Luddism and reopens the question
of just what can appropriately be categorised as Luddism.
This evidence can be examined without any assumption that
all testimony to the revolutionary features of the movement
is necessarily false; the accounts must be judged as they
stand.[12]

The first evidence to be looked at is that linked directly with
machine-breaking; this material is not extensive in quantity.
It includes a threatening letter sent to a Huddersfield owner

F

of shearing-frames which gave the man his orders to take down
the frames but also took the opportunity to inform him that
there were '2,782 Sworn Heroes . . . in the Army of Huddersfield alone'; these were linked with even greater numbers from
various specified places in the woollen and cotton areas and
with the weavers in Glasgow and other parts of Scotland. All
these men would rise up hoping 'for assistance from the French
Emperor in shaking off the yoke of the Rottenest, wickedest
and most Tyrannical Government that ever existed', replacing
it by a 'just Republic'. The declaration ended by stating that
arms would not be laid down until the House of Commons
had passed an 'Act to put down all the Machinery hurtfull to
the Commonality', which represented a somewhat less frightening and more constitutional climax to the campaign than that
hinted at in the earlier passages of the communication. It suggests that appropriate legislation regarding machinery was all
that was required by the writer of the letter and that the note
was padded out with spurious, hair-raising detail to put across
the particular point as forcibly as possible. Certainly there is
no good reason to suppose that Huddersfield contained '2,782
Sworn Heroes'.

Probably from the same pen came the address 'To all Croppers, Weavers, etc. and the Public at large' which called for
armed volunteers to help the redressers shake off their yoke
by following the noble example of the 'Brave Citizens of
Paris'; '40,000 Heroes are ready to break out', it was stated,
'to crush the Old Government and establish a New one'. This
missive talked only vaguely about 'wrongs' and 'tyranny' with
no specific reference to Luddite grievances; while there is no
reason to doubt that it was anything other than a genuine
Luddite statement, there seems every reason to suppose that it
was a stirring and joyous playing with words rather than a
serious call to arms or an accurate statement of Luddite
numbers and intentions. A further Luddite appeal was made
in a notice pinned up and addressed 'To Whitefield Luddites';
it urged them to be ready to join the army of revolution.
This was sent to London from the Manchester police office to

support the contention that the directors of the revolutionary proceedings had their headquarters at Manchester and that their confederacy was called 'The Northern National Army'. There is no ground for connecting this with machine-breaking, except the fact that the framers of the notice chose to use the term currently in vogue, and there is no entry made by the 'Northern National Army' into the Luddite story at any other point.[13]

Perhaps the most suggestive account of Luddism's tie-up with revolutionary politics comes from Frank Peel, whose Luddite annals have recently achieved fair respectability as a historical source and guardian of the 'oral tradition'. Peel describes a supposed visit by a Nottingham delegate called Weightman to Halifax, where Weightman tells of the 'thousands of weapons collected and stout arms to wield them', and calls on the croppers to join the stockingers in their insurrectionary plans. Nottingham, said Weightman, was in daily communication with societies in other centres of disaffection and was urging a general rising in May. Unfortunately, this historical reconstruction is so wild and inaccurate that it is as unacceptable as a general indication of the situation as it is on the specific detail. Weightman spoke of the shooting of Luddite John Westley at Arnold; in fact he was shot at Bulwell, an unthinkable confusion for a Nottingham man. This same George Weightman was said by Peel to have been involved in the Pentrich Rebellion of 1817 and subsequently acquitted with thirty others; in fact George Weightman was condemned to death along with Brandreth, Ludlam, and Turner, respited just before execution, and later transported. Also, many years later an aged villager recalled to the local historian John Neal that he had been acquainted with Weightman, who 'could not have been better behaved' up to the time of Pentrich, which seems a more zealous guardianship of the oral tradition than Peel managed on this point.[14]

There are several depositions made by prisoners which have to be considered in this context. One is that of Thomas Broughton of Barnsley, who turned informer and supplied

information about oath-taking and the supposed revolutionary
organisation which existed throughout the North. At best it
can be said, and has been said, that 'it is next to impossible
to sort out truth and falsehood from this'; but even this view
of Broughton's information overlooks the fact that Broughton
is claiming to be reporting only what he has heard and not
what he knows. Broughton may indeed have heard what he
reported, but this does not distinguish his evidence from the
rest of the hearsay and rumour that circulated. Broughton had
heard that there were 8,000 almost complete in arms in and
around Sheffield. He had heard that delegates had been at
Barnsley from Manchester and Stockport (he had only *heard*
this though he was himself a Barnsley man), and he had heard
of great numbers of Luddites at Huddersfield and Halifax and
of 7-8,000 at Leeds. He had further heard that the Luddites
intended 'ultimately to overturn the System of Government by
revolutionising the Country', and he thought that if a revolution occurred Burdett and Cartwright would join it. He had,
in other words, heard pretty much what practically everyone
was hearing at this time, but he could provide no ground for
believing that what was being heard was accurate or even
vaguely indicative of the nature of the situation. It may well be
that Broughton had taken part in some political association with
some Barnsley weavers, but that tells us nothing about the
Luddites. Barnsley was well outside the machine-breaking
area, and Broughton was not able to show that it featured in
its activities.[15]

More useful documents are the confession of Thomas
Whittaker and his earlier letter to the governor of Chester
Castle, where he awaited trial prior to conviction and transportation for administering illegal oaths; for these contain a
man's testimony of his own experience, connecting trade-union
activity with machine-breaking and later with more general
law-breaking. But here again the political content of the statements, the reference to drilling companies, the general-rising
plans that are well advanced in Yorkshire and Nottinghamshire, and the schemes for securing key places in London,

derives from a travelling delegate who visited Whittaker's meetings from outside rather than from Whittaker's own experiences. It is important to note that, as the Hammonds suggest, Whittaker was at this time anxious to ingratiate himself with the authorities and was offering his services, in return for his freedom, in the uncovering of existing conspiratorial organisations. The better his story, the more he could appear to offer the authorities and the greater his repentance would seem; yet he could offer no promise of insurrectionary conspiracies to be uncovered. He produced a highly colourful account of 'Riot Plunder Assasination [*sic*] and every thing subversive to the Laws of civilised Nations', and suggested that 'the Country is verging fast into a state of Anarchy and Confusion', but this was to offer no more than an exaggerated, extreme view of what was in fact so; the horrors he listed were demonstrably present, if in milder form. Whittaker was from the heart of revolution country, yet he failed to suggest any knowledge of revolutionary conspiracy which might have made his offer to the authorities a more interesting proposition.[16]

Yet there still remains the 'blue-print' for revolution, the documents said to have been picked up from the road at the time of the Luddite attack on Foster's mill at Horbury, near Wakefield, containing addresses identical with those cited at Despard's trial. These are unmistakably plans for revolution, though rather vague ones in spite of the instructions laid down for the 'conductors' or local organisers of the revolution. It is interesting that these documents might have turned up on the scene of a Luddite attack, but it can hardly be argued from this possible tie-up with Luddism that the plans were in any way identified with Luddite aims. The 'flowery, liberterian rhetoric' employed was not language to rally Luddites, and the literary style suggests the pen of an upper-class dilettante rather than a working class revolutionary. Nor does the reference to 'your scrupulous respect for private opinion and private property' strike quite the right note to suggest harmony with Luddite intentions and techniques. There is no need to suspect either a plant or a forgery to reject these documents as worthless in throwing light upon the Luddites and their plans.[17]

Other evidence of insurrectionary intent seems to amount to little more than rumour and gossip, of which there was no shortage. On 23 May, for instance, the Home Secretary was sent an account of public-house gossip from Wigan; Bellingham's assassination of Perceval had met with popular approval, more such activity was called for, a complete repeal of all taxes was demanded, and so on. This was no more frightening than the case of John Burgess, who stood charged with having damned the king, the government and the court, and having said that Burdett should be king of England when the blow was struck in London and that he hoped the soldiers would join the rebels after the first battle. More specific details were provided by Joseph Johnson, a prisoner in Chester Castle awaiting transportation, who attempted to ingratiate himself with the authorities by passing on prison gossip and stories which he was allegedly told by fellow-prisoners, of 'parties in manufacturing Towns' who would 'rise under a pretence of the dearness of provisions' and would 'put to death all the manufacturers they could get hold of; set fire to all the manufactories they could get at', and 'liberate Gaols'; the country was divided into districts, the inhabitants divided into divisions, the parties armed, and 'every man has ten rounds of Ball cartridges'. John Schofield, on trial for murder at York, was also reported to have said that Huddersfield, like other places, had its armed body in readiness and that 'they might all start in a movement and overturn the government'. John Schofield might have said this, he might even have believed it, but this is very flimsy evidence that it was so.[18]

The most copious evidence for the revolution conspiracy theory is contained in the reports of 'B', the informer who worked for R. A. Fletcher of Bolton over many years and whose writings covered a vast amount of paper during the Luddite period. 'B', the villain of Lancashire Luddism in the Hammonds' account for his stories of oath-taking and wild allegations about a general rising, has recently been rehabilitated and restored to the dignity of 'plain informer', having been exonerated of the charge that he acted as a provocateur. Unfortunately, informers tended to be anything but 'plain' and this admittedly garrulous, somewhat stupid man still needs to have his evidence treated with some caution. There seems little reason, for instance, to trust his accounts of events in which he himself participated if his remaining accounts cannot be trusted. On the other hand, there is no reason to disbelieve that Bent was actively involved both in trade-union and political activities in Lancashire; what is queried is that he ever shows, as he very much attempts to show, acceptable evidence of being part of a revolutionary conspiracy linking different parts of Britain and intimately associated with Luddism. 'B', the Hammonds said, 'specialised in a "general rising" ', but his communications lay no basis for a belief that one was being seriously planned or that this was somehow associated with machine-breaking. Rather do they suggest that historians have been right to view with scepticism the writings of someone so wild and imaginative.

Perhaps the most remarkable thing about Bent is his continued capacity for eliciting belief even after being repeatedly proved wrong in the forecasts he made. Like present-day prophets of the ending of the world, who transfer their attention to some new date for Armageddon as each successive prophecy fails to be fulfilled, Bent audaciously ignored his past failures and concentrated on the next climactic point, predicted but never reached. And his own enthusiasm carried with him the credulous Fletcher, who, like Bent, never minded or never noticed being proved wrong about previous assertions, moving on instead to new and more outrageous ones. Some two months after the big moment for rebellion, 1 May, was over, Bent is still informing Fletcher, and Fletcher relaying the intelligence to the Home Secretary, that many delegates have visited him from the Lancashire-Cheshire border, where the Luddites have considerable arms, are under military discipline, and plan to start their armed uprising before the trial of the '38' Manchester reformers. Fletcher reveals an unbelievable naïveté, considering his experience, in offering to the Home Secretary information as trustworthy on the grounds that it came from 'B' and that 'B' assured Fletcher that it might be depended upon. Like the earlier rebellions, this one also failed to materialise.[19]

One of the strongest reasons for accepting the possibility that the Luddites contemplated armed insurrection has always been the undoubted fact that raids for arms were, especially in Yorkshire, a clearly recognisable feature of Luddism at a particular time, perhaps the main feature of the movement in the months of May and June. It would not be unreasonable to ask why, if they were not planning armed insurrection, the Luddites needed to arm themselves in this way. The assumption that the collection of arms meant only this was, in fact, made; the thefts suggested to two Huddersfield magistrates 'the Approach of some decisive Movement on the part of this numerous and formidable band': arms were being collected to overturn the government, and it was hardly reassuring for some thieves in Huddersfield to offer the enigmatic comment that the guns they were collecting 'they would bring back when the wars were over'. The precise nature of the wars they had in mind is not clear; but the authorities suspected they were not simply the wars against machinery.

Even in Nottinghamshire, the area of least political accusation against the Luddites, the Duke of Newcastle reported that it was known that there were orders at Birmingham for arms for the rioters. And, along with the notion of an armed populace, there developed the idea of secret arms dumps, stockpiles which could be tapped when the great day came and the workmen were called to spring to arms; this was an idea which continued to be handed down as part of the popular oral tradition. As early as 1 May it was suggested from Huddersfield that there was strong reason to suppose that arms had been secreted in nearby woods, and rumours continued to be rife throughout 1812, for some informers specialised in secret arms dumps just as others specialised in a general rising. The informer Barrowclough was most emphatic in his

disclosures, but General Maitland confessed the total inability of the military forces to locate the arms he talked of and
doubted whether any important information could be got
out of Barrowclough. Radcliffe had previously, without avail,
tried to capitalise on these disclosures. In the end the authorities gradually rejected belief in the existence of arms dumps,
and even Captain Raynes, of the Stirlingshire Militia,
who had a fine nose for conspirators and a great zest for
tracking them down, admitted in February 1813 that from
every enquiry he had made he could not learn of any arms
depot consisting of more than six or eight weapons. The arms
that were collected evidently remained in private hands, for
the total failure of the authorities then or since to locate the
supposed depots is a fairly strong reason for accepting the
improbability of their existence.[20]

The chronology of arms thefts and the way it fits into the
general pattern of Luddite development is important. The
first reports of arms thefts in Yorkshire, the principal centre
of this activity, do not arise until the very end of April; the
stealing of weapons was evidently not part of initial Luddite
strategy but a later response to changed circumstances. The
changed circumstances were that through April the Luddites
attempted to attack factories and suffered defeat at the hands
of the military, who showed themselves prepared to shoot.
Clearly the primitive pitchforks and hooks such as the Westhoughton crowds had carried were now irrelevant, and hammers and axes were no threat to the rifles and cannon that
William Cartwright mobilised in his defence at Rawfolds or
Horsfall mounted at Ottiwells mill, Huddersfield. Abortive
attacks had also involved deaths as well as failure. The men
who attended the Stones meetings prior to Westhoughton
might not have carried firearms and other offensive weapons,
as Oliver Nicholson testified, but they would have been
strongly inclined to do so after the Middleton experience
should a similar coup have been under contemplation. Nightly
thefts of arms in the Yorkshire area, especially around
Huddersfield, were a feature of May, though as late as 6 June

the *Leeds Mercury* was reporting the theft of firearms by force and intimidation as a new development of Luddism.[21]

The purpose of the arms thefts can now be alternatively explained. They did not begin until Luddites had been killed and until military arms had been used against them; Cartwright had drawn the first blood, and factories defended by arms would have to be attacked with them if they were to be attacked at all. This need had been anticipated by the hand-loom weavers in March, if Humphrey Yarwood is to be believed, for they had then resolved, while planning machine-breaking, 'to collect money to procure arms to repel force by force if hindered in the execution of their designs'. This made good sense, too, in the light of the experience of eighteenth-century machine-breakers, who had armed themselves in order to resist arrest, and accounts of the attack on mills at Rawdon in March state that the machine-breakers had pistols. The arms thefts, then, had an industrial purpose, to facilitate attacks on buildings, even to help in the destruction of machinery. They also apparently served many private purposes as the crime wave and general robbery set in through the summer and autumn of 1812. Arms-stealing and plunder continue, reported the *Leeds Mercury* on 20 June; they were classified together because they belonged together, the one promoting the other. By November Fitzwilliam was reporting that general plunder was now the motive behind the persistent thefts; arms were taken only if they happened to fall in the way of the thieves, for they were not now being specifically sought. It certainly seems unlikely that arms were being stolen to equip potential revolutionaries, though the *Leeds Mercury* suggested they were being stolen by spies to frame the Luddites on a political charge. On 11 July Sir Francis Wood, Deputy Lieutenant of the West Riding, sent an interesting communication to Fitzwilliam about the recent House of Commons Committee of Secrecy Report, which he felt to be based on the Lancashire, rather than the Yorkshire, situation. The principal threat in Yorkshire, he wrote, was the seizure of arms, not the possibility of insurrection, and the proposed suspension of Habeas Corpus would not help them on this matter. Clearly Wood had no fear of rebellion arising out of arms thefts: that would have been too logical an interpretation of the situation; there were other and better explanations.[22]

But it still remains to be asked what people really feared. Enormous numbers of soldiers were not stationed throughout the North and Midlands on account of the rantings and ravings of a few spies, and people in authority were not encouraging spies to provoke trouble to frighten themselves; they were not deliberately creating a problem out of nothing so that they could lose nights' sleep and days' rest on its solution, throwing the country into a panic all the while. Those in authority, whatever their mistaken judgement or class prejudices, were by and large not fools. There was a great fear in being, and it was not one that had been conjured out of thin air by spies or had sprung from the distempered spirit of some petty magistrate in a south Lancashire cotton town. It is suggested, however, that this fear was not so much a fear of political revolution as a fear of social anarchy or even a physical fear of attack on property and persons; political revolution was too sophisticated a concept for the Luddites and not the aim of most parliamentary reformers. Burdett might have liked the idea of some measure of radical political change if this could be done without any social revolution being involved. The Luddites on the other hand had only vague notions of social amelioration, and no concept of this as a consequence of political action and the use of political power. They gave general support to parliamentary reform, but acting politically meant for them striking a few blows, not organising a political campaign, let alone a revolution.

Just what did words like 'revolution' or 'insurrection' mean in the context of 1812? At the beginning of his rounds General Maitland was expressing his belief in 'a combination to overcome all legal authority' which aimed at 'nothing more or less than the subversion of the Government of the Country and the destruction of all Property', but at the same time as he was using this strong language he was also expressing his disbelief that an actual rising was seriously intended. Even when he continued to refer to what were described as 'revolutionary movements', he admitted that there were no plans for anything other than open acts of violence, that there were no definite objects or distinct ends for these so-called revolutionary movements. The government of the country was being subverted when its laws were being broken on a wide scale, and when this took place, particularly in the sphere of property rights, the movement was subversive to the point of being revolutionary. Outrages such as the attack on Rawfolds mill, according to the *Leeds Intelligencer,* 'affect the very vitals of society, whatever they are directed against', and in this sense the Luddites were revolutionary because they were choosing to ignore the customary mechanisms and procedures of society and attempting to right particular wrongs by rejecting one of society's most hallowed conventions, the sanctity of private property, which even kings had disturbed only at their peril.

It is probable that people were not sure what they feared and that their language was often in excess of the sentiments they were really experiencing. Richard Wood, the Borough Reeve of Manchester, wrote on 28 April that the great effort of the discontented was to be made some night of the following week, when they planned to attack the banks, the houses of the rich, and the barracks. This sounds like fear of a revolutionary movement, but Wood had nothing to say about the political purpose of these moves, how they were to be concerted with movements elsewhere, how they were to be directed against the government, and how they were to result in the transfer of political power. The banks, the houses of the rich, the barracks even, were all obvious targets for rioting crowds, with no particular significance to suggest, for instance, that a rebel movement was planning to take over the country's currency or its armed forces. It was insurrection against society that Wood was describing rather than insurrection against the government, and of this the Luddites and their fellow protesters were clearly guilty. Wood's forecasts were in fact very much along the same lines as an early prediction from Manchester that the labouring classes in that part of the country were determined on a 'General Riot'; if people in all the towns within a ten-mile radius were to rise up together, it was suggested, it would be quite a problem to put them down. Again, 'rise up' is a suggestive term, but it is evident from the discussion of a 'General Riot' that nothing more than rioting over a wide area was envisaged.[23]

In the slightly less confused situation in Yorkshire, though there were some, such as Dr Conisborough of Halifax, who said, and almost certainly meant and believed, that there was a 'deep laid System of organised Rebellion and Revolution' in existence, others were more careful to distinguish between the probable and the unlikely. The *Leeds Mercury* produced its account of the attack on Burton's mill at Middleton under the heading 'The New Era, the insurrectionary era', but the article itself indicated that no political connotation was understood and that the insurrection was no more than an attack on a mill, or some such enterprise. A more careful use of the term was by Dr Thompson, the Secretary of the Association Committee at Halifax, created to help the authorities, when he gave his view that the danger in Halifax was chiefly to individuals; riots or public disturbances were not likely, and insurrection was even less so. The 'disposition to popular commotion', which the *Leeds Mercury* had said had taken root in the West Riding by the end of March, certainly existed, but it was individuals who were its victims, not institutions or governments. Lord Fitzwilliam, writing to Mr Ryder at the Home Office on 16 May, could foresee nothing worse than outrage against individuals, for the mass of the people were, he believed, of sound disposition. And he was proved correct in his sanguine forecasts. The government was faced with nothing more serious than a problem of maintaining law and order. The insurgents who regularly drilled themselves by night were not, even in Home Office records, a revolutionary army preparing to strike against the government, for Ryder had said as early as 12 May that there was no real danger of insurrection, but workmen organising themselves for the next attack upon an offensive mill. By September even the politically 'disaffected' were said to be deriving their confidence from Cartwright and looking up to him as leader, which is a fair measure of their political disaffection and the short distance they would be led on the road to revolution.[24]

Unfortunately, it is not only nineteenth-century terminology but twentieth-century connotations also that lead to confusion; it is important to know if commentators are talking about the same thing before they disagree with each other on their conclusions. We are warned that Luddism was 'not a wholly conscious revolutionary movement', that rather it had a 'tendency towards becoming such a movement', but what was only a tendency and what an established characteristic is not always clear. In April and May 1812, for instance, Luddism is said to have become the focus of a 'diffused and confused insurrectionary tension', and the food riots and anonymous letters of April are said to have been the product of a 'sheer insurrectionary fury' which has rarely been more widespread in England. It is not clear if the tension and the fury meant that insurrection was genuinely being plotted, though it is later suggested that a revolutionary conspiracy extended beyond the manufacturing areas to places like Barnsley and Sheffield, where the Luddites were 'inspired by crude notions of upsetting the government' when sufficient arms had been collected. This view smacks a little of Frank Peel and his oral tradition, and it is difficult to see why the Sheffield crowds, in view of the alleged need to collect sufficient arms for a rebellion, should have thrown up the opportunity of acquiring them during the food riots of 14 April when they attacked the local militia arsenal but destroyed, rather than carried off, the weapons contained therein. We are rightly cautioned against too dogmatic and firm an interpretation of Luddite schemes, but when we are warned that Luddism was a movement with 'no national objectives beyond . . . the desire to overturn the government' this sounds like a soft sell for a very hard line. The allegation is no highest common factor present in all interpretations but a highly tendentious view to be found amongst alarmists and provocateurs. The cool-headed would have none of it.[25]

The 'failure of imagination' which has allegedly caused most serious examinations of Luddism to distinguish between the industrial aims which the machine-breakers pursued and the political ones which the alarmists ascribed to them, has afflicted more than academics; it was experienced, too, by cool-headed administrators such as Fitzwilliam, whose job it was to deal with Luddism. Ralph Fletcher of Bolton and his informer Bent were clearly not lacking in imagination though a little weak in judgement, but it is the task of the historian to put their exaggerations into perspective and not to enhance them. It is intolerable licence to maintain that the connection between machine-breaking and political sedition was assumed on every side, even in Nottingham. Rather is the contrary true, that in this town the activity of machine-breaking was considered by all but a hair-raising minority to be a matter entirely separate and distinct from politics. Certainly Nottingham, like other places, produced its funny stories; it was particularly good at conjuring up imaginary Frenchmen who disbursed money amongst the rioters, and libelling national figures for whom Luddism was a mere front; and the Duke of Newcastle even heard of arms consignments which poured in from Birmingham, that inevitable arsenal for supplying all intent on political mischief. But never a shred of evidence for these tales was produced. Police officers Conant and Baker from London investigated the charges and found them totally without foundation; Luddism, according to the *Nottingham Review,* had nothing to do with politics; it was, in the words of town clerk George Coldham, 'a question entirely distinct from all feelings of party spirit or attachment or disaffection to the State, Administration etc'.[26]

If the proof of the revolution pudding was to be in the eating, the gastric juices of the alarmists were never to be stimulated, for the pudding never appeared on the table. That an event never occurred is not necessarily proof that none was ever planned, for history is full of such abortions, but it seems a not unfair test of the interpretations of Luddism offered on the one side by Ralph Fletcher and his informant Bent, and on the other by Lord Fitzwilliam and General Maitland, to ask which party was vindicated by events. The passing of weeks made the alarmist predictions seem increasingly silly and the passing of a century and a half has not made them appear any more sensible. By contrast, the moderate words and optimistic predictions of Maitland and Fitzwilliam about the course that Luddism would run and the way it would peter out were borne out in a manner that imparts to their opinions a validity and reasonableness that have not been seriously challenged.

1   Report of Select Committee on Artizans and Machinery, 1824, v, p 280; Felkin, W. *History of the Machine Wrought Hosiery* . . . . p 230
2   Newcastle MSS Ne C4920, Thomas Large to Newcastle, 26 March 1812; HO 42/117, Newcastle to HO, 29 December 1811; Ne C4919b, Becher to Newcastle, 12 February 1812; HO 42/119, Middleton to HO, 11 January 1812; HO 42/117, Coldham to HO, (December) 1811; Nottingham Borough Records, M429, F16
3   eg HO 42/119, Coldham to HO, 14 January 1812
4   Thompson, E. P. *The Making* . . . . pp 548-9
5   Ibid pp 542-543
6   Radcliffe MSS 126/26, 126/27; HO 40/1, Statement of H. Yarwood, 22 June 1812; *Leeds Intelligencer,* 27 April 1812; HO 40/1, Lloyd to HO, 2 May 1812; Hutton to HO, 1 May 1812
7   Radcliffe MSS 126/38; *Leeds Mercury,* 9 January 1813; HO 42/122, Grey to HO, 20 April 1812, Campbell to Grey, 16 April 1812; HO 40/1, Huddersfield Secret Committee to HO, 29 April 1812; Wood to HO, 7 June 1812; Thompson, E. P. *The Making* . . . . pp 572, 590, 601
8   HO 42/124, Maitland to HO, 30 June 1812; Thompson, E. P. *The Making* . . . . p 569; HO 40/1, Lloyd to HO, 17 June 1812
9   Read, D. *Manchester Guardian,* 2 October 1956; Thompson, E. P. *The Making* . . . . pp 599-600
10 HO 42/122, G. Hadfield to HO, 20 April 1812; HO 40/1,

H. D. Broughton to HO, 27 April 1812; TS 11/980, 3580;
Raynes, F. *An Appeal to the Public*, containing an account of
services rendered during the disturbances in the North of England in the year 1812 (1817) p 58; HO 42/122, Flixton to HO,
19 April 1812, Lees to HO, 23 April 1812; HO 40/1,
Fletcher to HO, 26 April 1812; HO 42/125, York letter of
15 July 1812; HO 42/123, W. Chippendale to HO, 22 May
1812; J. Wigfull to HO, 17 May 1812

11 HO 42/123, Maitland to HO, 4, 6, 23 May 1812; HO 42/124,
Précis of General Maitland's communication from Manchester,
19 June 1812; HO 42/126, Maitland to HO, 22, 24 August
1812; *Leeds Mercury*, 23 January 1813; *Nottingham Review*,
23 January 1818; Fitzwilliam MSS 46/68

12 Thompson, E. P. *The Making* .... pp 592-3

13 HO 40/1, 'Ned Ludd' to Mr Smith, undated; Ibid; HO 40/122,
Police Office, Manchester, to HO, 27 April 1812.

14 Peel, F. *The Risings of the Luddites* pp 25-7; Neal, J. *The
Pentrich Revolution* (1966 edn) p 104

15 Fitzwilliam MSS 46/122; Thompson, E. P. *The Making* ....
pp 578-9.

16 HO 42/121, Deposition of Thomas Whittaker, 4 July 1812;
HO 42/123, Whittaker to the Governor of Chester Castle,
undated; Hammond, J. L. and B. *The Skilled Labourer* p 274

17 HO 40/1; Thompson, E. P. *The Making* .... p 598

18 HO 42/123; HO 42/127, Details of persons committed to
York; HO 40/1, Information of Joseph Johnson, 10, 12, 13
May 1812; *Leeds Mercury*, 9 January 1813

19 Thompson, E. P. *The Making* .... pp 593, 594; Hammond,
J. L. and B. *The Skilled Labourer* p 275; HO 42/124, Fletcher
to HO, 30 June 1812

20 HO 40/1, Scott and Armitage to HO, 2 May 1812; Ibid,
Huddersfield Secret Committee to HO, 29 April 1812; HO
42/120, Newcastle to HO, 29 February 1812; HO 42/123,
Gordon to General Grey, 1 May 1812; HO 42/125, Maitland
to HO, 20 July 1812; HO 40/2, F. Raynes to HO, 7 February
1813

21 TS 11/980, 3580; HO 42/128, Deposition of O. Nicholson;
Leeds Mercury, 6 June 1812

22 HO 40/1, Deposition of H. Yarwood, 22 June 1812; *Leeds
Mercury*, 28 March 1812; Rudé, G. *The Crowd in History*
p 73; HO 42/129, Fitzwilliam to HO, 2 November 1812; *Leeds
Mercury*, 25 July 1812; Fitzwilliam MSS 46/23

23 HO 42/123, Maitland to HO, 4, 6 May 1812; *Leeds Intelli-*
G

gencer, 20 April 1812; HO 42/122, Wood to HO, 28 April 1812; HO 42/121, Dinsdale to HO, 30 March 1812

24 Fitzwilliam MSS 45/141, 45/142, 46/1, 46/9; *Leeds Mercury*, 25 April, 28 March 1812; HO 40/2, Raynes to HO, 21 September 1812

25 Thompson, E. P. *The Making* . . . . pp 553, 564, 570, 591, 599

26 Thompson, E. P. *The Making* . . . . pp 577, 587; HO 42/120, Newcastle to HO, 29 February 1812; Ibid, Conant and Baker to HO, 6 February 1812; *Nottingham Review*, 23 January 1818; HO 42/138, Coldham to HO, 7 April 1812

Chapter Four

THE ORGANISATION
OF LUDDISM

IT IS NOT simply the problem of determining Luddite aims that focuses attention on the nature of Luddite organisation, but also the technical success of machine-breaking, a success which suggests that the enterprise was in places thoroughly well organised. At its inception in March 1811, machine-breaking seems to have been no more than an extended form of rioting, with demonstrating crowds giving vent to their feelings and drawing attention to their specific grievances by breaking the stocking-frames of hosiers whose conduct was offensive to them. On 11 March some hundreds of framework-knitters, supposedly from the country districts, assembled in Nottingham market-place, and speeches were made protesting at the treatment they were receiving. The constables were called out and a troop of Dragoons paraded until nine o'clock in the evening. Later the stockingers marched off to Arnold, north of the town, and broke over sixty stocking-frames there, dispersing before the arrival of the Dragoons the next morning. When frame-breaking was revived in the autumn, the Luddites were still numbered in their hundreds; on one occasion a thousand were said to have assembled for action, and with this degree of popular involvement there remained an informality and spontaneity which were later lacking. Gradually the numbers directly participating fell, though there might still be, according to Blackner, any number from six to sixty involved according to the nature of the job

to be done. These parties accepted the absolute authority of
their leader, their General Ludd; he placed armed guards to
cover the rest, while those equipped with hammers and axes
were commanded to enter the house or workshop concerned
to smash the frames. Afterwards a roll was called, with the
men answering to a number rather than a name, and the signal
was then given for departure by the firing of a pistol. Other
accounts mention the assembling of the parties on the fringes
of the forest beyond the town to the north, and describe the
set procedure followed there before the attacks were actually
launched. It is very clear that, once Luddism proceeded beyond
the stage of being almost a spontaneous outburst of popular
indignation, it became a well-drilled and regimented operation,
executed with a technical competence that left the peace-
keeping authorities gasping.[1]

But Nottinghamshire Luddism moved a stage beyond even
this professionalism. It has been suggested that the limited
frame-breaking of the winter of 1812-13 was the work of one
small gang of experts, and it is clear that Luddism in its final
stages in 1816 was very much a job done for money. When a
particular operation was decided upon, gangs were recruited to
execute the work, and certain individuals would make their
public-house contacts, discussing the nature of the enterprise,
the terms being offered, and the precise details for arming
and assembling the gang. John Blackburn, who said he had
been offered £40 for the Loughborough attack on Heathcoat's
mill, somewhat whimsically commented that the spirit present
in the early stage of Luddism was not there in the later stage.
The real professionals had taken over from those who had
started out breaking machines in the belief that they were
benefiting the trade; now it was personal benefit that counted.
Sutton wrote that without funds there would have been little
destruction of machinery, and Felkin that it was done for
hire. The problem of identifying the source of the money
believed to have changed hands over machine-breaking remains
to be considered.[2]

There was a similar progression from spontaneous popular

protest to an ever-increasing degree of organisation and professionalism in Yorkshire Luddism also, though the professionalism here was a matter of competence rather than of being paid to do a job. The first evidence that Luddism had spread to the West Riding occurred on the night of Wednesday, 15 January 1812, when the magistrates of Leeds had to disperse a crowd of men with blackened faces, arresting one of them, after receiving information that a conspiracy was afoot to destroy the machinery of certain mills; the black-faced crowd and the subsequent firing of Oatlands Mill the following Sunday gave some substance to the conspiracy allegation. By late February, organisation had emerged. On the night of 22 February attacks were made on two dressing-shops in Huddersfield; it was reported that the Luddites were divided into two parties, with the most daring and expert doing the job while others kept watch. After it was over the leader called a roll, the men answered to numbers, pistols were fired, shouts were raised, and the men marched off in regular military order. The Nottinghamshire pattern was being repeated almost exactly.

Very soon the Yorkshire Luddites were moving on towards bigger targets than the dressing-shops, and mounting attacks upon full-scale factories: this necessarily involved bigger numbers and greater problems. Josiah Foster of Horbury, whose father's factory was attacked in mid-April, wrote an interesting account of the episode, in which he emphasised two noteworthy points about the behaviour of the attackers. In spite of the fact that they were several hundred in number, they did not wander over the factory breaking machines at random as they went; instead they bypassed the scribbling machines 'which when they saw they said they were not what they wanted for the machines they wanted were the cropping machines'. Also, though several shots were fired during the attack, it was not believed that killing or even injuring anyone was intended, for the breaking of windows was the only damage that resulted. A few days later occurred the Yorkshire classic, the attack on Cartwright's mill at Rawfolds, when the Luddites assembled near the Dumb Steeple at Mirfield, were called over and regimented in a field, and marched over Hightown into the Spen Valley for an abortive onslaught in which two of their number were killed. Just as the Horbury attackers had been seen dispersing in the various directions of Wakefield, Leeds, Halifax and Huddersfield once their mission was complete, so the Rawfolds army was similarly built up from districts of Huddersfield and Halifax and the villages of Spen Valley. Leeds too was expected to provide a sizeable contingent, but it arrived late and returned home without participating in the conflict. The planning of these enterprises, involving some hundreds of men, clearly demanded more organisation than any 'spontaneous college rag'; on the other hand the staging of such an enterprise within a relatively small and compact geographical area cannot be used to demonstrate the contacts and co-operation of conspirators over three counties, a tightly-knit organisation bound together by a secret oath, or a political purpose. The attacks of the croppers are sufficiently explicable within the immediate context of the geographical and industrial environment of the cloth trade.[3]

In Lancashire the degree of organisation and evidence of technical competence observable elsewhere seem to be lacking, which is a little ironical in that the attacks on steam-looms were in part the outcome of a specific decision taken by already existing organisations of the weavers, who thought that this different technique might be a supplement to, or substitute for, methods previously tried. Though there are several accounts of meetings of the trade which discussed the promotion of machine-breaking in Lancashire and North Cheshire, there is little in the actual machine-breaking that occurred to show that it resulted from the planning and organisation previously achieved. The attacks on Radcliffe's warehouse at Stockport in March, the attempt to fire Marsland's factory in February, and the attack on Goodair's property during the Stockport riots of mid-April, all appear to arise from popular commotion, which might or might not have been specifically instigated and given direction by the existing trade committees. Similarly, the attacks on Burton's mill at Middleton on 20 and 21 April were mass enterprises involving many hundreds, perhaps more than a thousand men, whose great numbers and various occupations suggest that they were not a deliberately planned and contrived attacking force. And in the case of Westhoughton it was apparently only when popular protest took over from carefully planned intrigue by the Bolton spies that the long-threatened attack upon the establishment was finally accomplished. The plans, deliberations and achievements of the Nottinghamshire and Yorkshire machine-breakers might indicate a high degree of organisation, but the very limited and chaotically-planned machine-breaking of Lancashire and Cheshire suggests highly defective organisation or lack of serious intent to proceed in this particular way.[4]

The actual numbers involved in individual attacks have been a matter of some dispute. In Nottinghamshire the early days of machine-breaking by riot probably involved as many as two or three hundred people, but as the organisation and planning took over, much smaller bodies were detailed to perform particular jobs, though cases of individual workmen sabotaging the machinery for which they were working and for which they were personally responsible were frequently suspected. Such smaller groups were probably involved in most of the Yorkshire attacks on houses or cropping-shops; it is over the major attacks on factories that numbers become difficult to estimate. Josiah Foster thought that about six hundred men had taken part in the Horbury attack, though local press and other reports suggested about half that number. Estimates of the numbers present at Rawfolds Mill suggested up to three hundred, but again half that number is more likely. The *Leeds Intelligencer*, unable to arrive at a precise figure, suggested that the fact that only two men fell was a fairly clear indication that the ranks were not very closely filled up, while Cartwright himself said he had no clear idea of the numbers involved, though the guard outside the door had estimated that between one and two hundred men were present. Peel suggested that the number was about 150, some fifty short of expectation because of Leeds defections, and this guess is probably near enough to the truth.

It is even more difficult to estimate the numbers involved in the Lancashire episodes because of their confused nature and because most of them arose out of popular riots where the numbers could be anything. On the occasion of the Dean Moor meeting of 19 April, when an attack on Westhoughton was intended at the instigation of Stones, there were, according to state briefs, some eighty or ninety present, a figure probably based on Ralph Fletcher's admission that there were less than a hundred there. Arrested men who had actually been present varied in their estimates from thirty to sixty; forty seems to have been the most popular guess, and of these probably a dozen were spies. One prisoner, Oliver Nicholson, alleged that prior to Dean Moor not more than twenty men had attended any one of their meetings. When Lancashire Luddism, like that of Yorkshire, lapsed into arms thefts, the precise size of the parties involved is no less difficult to determine; according to Lloyd of Stockport bodies of one hundred men were entering houses night after night to seize arms, but this seems improbable for reasons already discussed.[5]

One further aspect of Luddite behaviour warrants more consideration: the reputation the Luddites enjoyed, by and large, for being respecters of private property outside the range of machines and materials which were offensive to them as workmen. This good name the Luddites largely owed to the early period of their activities; when the *Leeds Mercury* forecast that frame-breaking was opening the door for the commission of every other species of crime, it identified one of the real dangers in machine-breaking. The decline of Nottinghamshire Luddism into robbery, thuggery, attempted murder, and general violence vindicated this opinion, as did the similar decline in Yorkshire. But even earlier the Luddites were enjoying a reputation perhaps slightly in excess of their deserts. The Huddersfield attacks of 22 February might have been notable for their freedom from mischief to other species of property and for the gentle treatment of individuals involved, but there were examples of quite different behaviour. Thompson and Son at Rawdon had thirty-six windows broken and three pieces of fine woollen cloth destroyed on 23 March, a Leeds firm had eighteen pieces of cloth destroyed two nights later, and the Huddersfield firm of Vickerman had wool set on fire as well as having their cropping-shears destroyed. It was here that one Luddite made his classic utterance that Ned Ludd of Nottingham had ordered him to break the clock in the owner's house, a gratuitous piece of destructive behaviour which did not help the cause. Following Rawfolds and the murder of Horsfall, whatever reservations were held about private personal property as opposed to industrial property disappeared in the general thieving that developed, particularly of arms and money. Again, generalisations about Nottinghamshire and Yorkshire Luddites break down somewhat in Lancashire, where machine-breaking was less a question of raids on private property, during which temptation was often avoided, and more a question of general riotous behaviour which involved attacks on the fabric of houses and the firing of warehouses as well as the singling-out of machinery for destruction. Lancashire Luddism did not have its 'pure' period.[6]

The problem of identifying the Luddites, that is determining the social composition of the movement, inescapably resurrects the problem of definition. It is not satisfactory to characterise the Luddites on the basis of those men who were arrested for, accused, and convicted of food rioting or even administering illegal oaths. The York prisoners of January 1813 might indeed have been of all occupations, but they were not all Luddites. If it is agreed to call all forms of law-breaking Luddism, it is easy enough to find all sorts of people amongst the Luddites. The Macclesfield rioters of 15 April might have consisted of colliers, carters and spinners, and the Manchester and Leeds food rioters of women and children, but this does not throw light upon the machine-breakers. More to the point is the letter sent by W. Chippendale, in command of the militia at Oldham, to the Home Secretary on 21 April, in which he described the several hundred colliers who had descended upon the town with picks 'for the purpose of sapping my little fortress' for arms before going back to Middleton and using their specific skills to perforate the walls of Burton's factory there which contained steam-looms. But even this was essentially a popular riot in which discontent focused upon the obvious target in the area, and the discontented included men other than those for whom steam-looms were a real, personal grievance. The presence among the dead of a baker, a glazier and a joiner need occasion no surprise.[7]

Peel's view of the Luddites was that they were not all croppers but included within their ranks weavers, tailors, shoemakers, representatives, in fact, of almost every craft; they were people who had in common that they were on the brink of starvation and desperation; he also noted that part of the movement were the uneducated and brutal, who found it more pleasurable to steal by violence than to earn by industry. This second opinion is probably based on Luddism as it degenerated into general thieving through the late spring and summer; the first, a more suggestive comment, probably derives from Peel's assumption, which may or may not be correct, that the political radicals such as Baines the hatter, of Halifax, were involved in Luddite councils and might therefore be properly termed Luddites. If the term is to be applied to the political radicals amongst the working classes, then it would be surprising if a large range of occupational groups was not to be found in the ranks. If, on the other hand, the machine-breakers only are to be so identified, and in a context of industrial action rather than popular riot, there seems little reason for supposing that the breakers of shearing-frames and gig-mills were not croppers and cloth-dressers and the breakers of stocking and lace frames not framework-knitters. Certainly all the people charged with these offences belonged to the occupations concerned in the operation of the machinery destroyed. It is tempting to see Luddism as a movement of working-class solidarity, with different occupational groups coming to the assistance of the specifically-oppressed groups who are campaigning against and breaking machinery, but this can only be shown if it is acceptable that all the different forms of popular protest in being in 1812 are appropriate to be called Luddism. What can be and has been shown is that the Luddites operated against a background of considerable popular sympathy; the Midlands framework-knitters were always able to enlist strong middle- and lower-middle-class support for their industrial and political campaigns, and the Midlands Luddites clearly enjoyed a large measure of protection from the society in which they lived. The same is equally true of the West Riding croppers, but this is different from a suggestion that Luddism was organised and perpetrated by the working class as distinct from certain groups within it.

Precise details are, of course, impossible to come by, and there is a natural reluctance to generalise from particular cases, but it is interesting to note that of the thirty-nine people who came before Fitzwilliam's magistrates from Huddersfield, Raistrick, Hipperholme and Birstall to take advantage of the Prince Regent's amnesty to those who had taken secret oaths, three were miners, one a cobbler, and thirty-five textile workers, though what sort of oaths these persons were supposed to have taken is not clear. Whatever the fringe involvement in Luddism of working-class groups other than textile workers, it seems impossible to doubt the accuracy of the Home Office view that the whole movement was limited to the 'very lowest orders of the people', which gave the authorities great comfort since they doubted very much whether the 'lowest orders' were on their own capable of giving a serious political challenge to the government. Peel, also, believed that better-class workmen held aloof from Luddism and that this fact left the movement short of leaders.[8]

A somewhat romantic attempt has been made to characterise the men who 'organised, sheltered, or condoned Luddism' as literate, humorous, and politically-experienced, by transferring to the body of Luddites qualities found among the framework-knitters who organised the 1812 petition to Parliament. Apart from being logically indefensible, this is also a mischievous operation, for it apparently makes these framework-knitters guilty, by association, of Luddism, a most unfortunate conclusion to arrive at when the evidence of their correspondence indicates just how strong was their resentment of it.[9]

Other things that can be said about the Luddites are that they were young men, in their late teens or early twenties in the case of many of those unfortunate enough to be caught, and that they were invariably said to be strangers to the area in which they operated and from which they were reported. No one wanted to own them; like the Reform Bill rioters of 1831 in Nottingham and Bristol, or trouble-makers in general, they were always strangers or from a neighbouring village; we have no apprehension about our neighbours, wrote Joseph Priestley from Halifax on 18 May; our dangers arise from Huddersfield and Lancashire, and it was usually so whenever a person reported on the troubles of his own locality.[10]

Some attempt must now be made to answer the question of how numerous the Luddites actually were, and it is not difficult to find plenty of support for the contradictory propositions that they were very numerous and that they were very few. The House of Commons Committee of Secrecy inclined to the view that they were 'considerable', but accompanied this with a warning that there was in fact no satisfactory evidence of the numbers involved. The evidence consisted almost entirely of the guesses and hunches of particular persons, and greater credence can be given to those people who appear most capable of taking a balanced and realistic view of the situation and have least emotional involvement, though who remained balanced and realistic in his judgements is still a matter of opinion. An account that maintains, dogmatically, that it was ascertained that 12,000 had taken 'the oath' is wrong; such might have been the case, but it was not ascertained to be so. Similarly with the 2,782 sworn heroes in the army of Huddersfield, the 40,000 'sworn in to do their best in the counties of Nottinghamshire, Leicestershire, and Derbyshire' or 'the 56,000 who could be relied upon' from the Glasgow area; the foundations for these claims were never disclosed; the number sworn in, wrote Ralph Wright of Flixton, was 'said to be enormous', but he did not inform his reader who had said so and how the verdict had been reached.

Nor is it very helpful to learn that the *Leeds Mercury* did not apprehend the persons in the lawless combination to be so numerous as some supposed, except as an indication that disagreement existed on the issue. The high estimates of Luddite strength were derived either from the reports of spies who, despite their recent rehabilitation, were by the nature of their calling alarmist and had a vested interest in magnifying the problem, or from the boasts or threats of Luddites, for whom the bigger the boast or the threat the better the effect they expected to produce. The low estimates, on the other hand, came from people who were just as much concerned with the problem of the preservation of law and order as R. A. Fletcher of Bolton or J. Lloyd of Stockport, but who were capable of taking a broader view of the situation because of the greater scope of their position and who did not rely on spies for the information. Fitzwilliam, the Lord Lieutenant of the West Riding, was in contact with magistrates throughout his area of jurisdiction and received a large correspondence from people who felt they had matters of importance to communicate to him. Throughout the crisis Fitzwilliam remained cool and never panicked; he was always very careful to analyse precisely the nature of the problem facing the authorities, and remained convinced throughout that the great mass of the people continued to be well disposed and law-abiding. By 14 August he was writing that 'the mischievous'—for he rated them no more seriously than that at this point—were very limited in numbers; and his careful appraisal of the causes of popular discontent and his predictions about its decline suggest that he was one of the most reliable of contemporary commentators.

Another whose judgement must be respected is General Maitland, who, like Fitzwilliam, tried to place the statements of the spies and alarmists in perspective and whose fears declined as his knowledge and experience increased. From the

start he could find no general inclination to support the Luddites, whatever sympathy they might be receiving, and it was on
the basis of his reports that the Home Secretary accepted that
Luddism was very much a 'minority movement'. By late
August Maitland was confirming that everything he saw was
leading him to believe that numbers were even smaller than
he had previously imagined, and his imagination had never run
riot. His confident mood remained when he crossed over into
Yorkshire; although fewer than fifty there had taken advantage
of the royal proclamation, this was, he believed, because so few
people had been involved in oath-taking. Earlier, the Treasury
Solicitor, Henry Hobhouse, had supplied London with the
encouraging opinion that the prisoners to be tried at York
for the most notorious cases of Luddite offences appeared to
have been 'the principal actors in the greater part of the other
outrages'. In other words, the active Luddites had been so few
that the troubles would stop when the ring-leaders were taken,
which is what happened.[11]

However numerous or few the Luddites were, their methods
of operation were certainly such as to indicate to the authorities a high degree of efficiency in their organisation. 'The
secrecy with which the plans of the disaffected are carried on',
wrote a member of the Manchester police office, 'is scarcely
credible', and it was the same story elsewhere. The manner
and secrecy of the system, wrote Colonel Campbell to General
Grey, were rendering ineffectual all the efforts of the authorities to suppress Yorkshire Luddism; and in Nottinghamshire
both borough and county magistrates found from the earliest
days that enormous sums of money were proving quite ineffective as a means of buying their way into Luddite secrets.
It was, in the Home Office view, the Nottinghamshire system
of organisation that extended itself to the northern counties,
acquiring in the process a slightly different character and
more violent attributes.[12]

It is impossible to reject the view that the successful raids
mounted in different parts of the country could not have been
staged without proficient organisation, though it is less easy

to be sure about the exact form that such organisation took. Henry Hardie of Manchester, for instance, was convinced that masonic lodges were providing the organisation and cover for Luddism, and he sought the Home Secretary's approval to have all lodges searched for the incriminating evidence. The more generally accepted view was that of the House of Commons Committee of Secrecy, which saw the 'organised system of unlawful violence' as emanating from a complex structure of local committees, secret committees, and executive committees, with regular links and communication maintained through delegates who travelled to and fro and attended meetings. These delegates, according to the House of Lords' Secret Committee, were being 'continually dispatched from one place to another for the purpose of concerting plans'. The whole business was believed to have almost the structure of a Presbyterian system of church organisation, with comparable efficiency and of comparable menace to the State with that felt by Elizabeth 250 years earlier.[13]

This view of Luddite organisation, and it is a view which has been popularly accepted, appears to derive very largely from Lancashire sources; it is a view which men such as Fletcher and Lloyd were picking up from the reports of spies, especially Bent, and which seemed to be confirmed by the confessions and depositions of informers and repentants such as Whittaker and Yarwood. But it is probably an exaggerated view of the real situation; the spies were deliberately hairraising in their utterances, and the informers were almost certainly deluded as to the real extent of the network of which they had been part. Five years later, over the Pentrich rebellion, a few men in the North and Midlands persuaded themselves, through a delegate network, that they controlled a powerful organisation, ready to be mobilised for rebellion, but their beliefs were shown to be illusions. Similarly, the men who tramped between Stockport, Manchester and Bolton, as trade-union representatives or to carry word of a machinebreaking conspiracy to a small audience of workmen, were probably under a delusion about the strength of those for

whom and to whom they spoke. The healthily sceptical Maitland was quick to form the opinion in Lancashire that the
Luddites were not in the state of organisation believed by
many and that their machinery was not in an advanced state
of development.[14]

It is much easier to accept Peel's account of a much more
informal kind of contact that developed among the croppers
at the Shears' Inn, Hightown; here, on Saturday evenings,
croppers from the Spen Valley and just beyond were said to
get together, and it was here, supposedly, that they were regaled
by tales from William Hall, who came back to his Liversedge
home at weekends, but who worked during the week at John
Wood's cropping-shop at Huddersfield, where Joseph Mellor
and others later hanged for the murder of William Horsfall
also worked. This kind of contact in this kind of environment
is perfectly credible as a means by which the Luddites of one
place heard of doings elsewhere and planned co-operative
enterprises for the future, and it was almost certainly in this
way that great enterprises such as the Horbury and Rawfolds
mill attacks were arranged. These affairs certainly demanded
a few individuals of authority who were capable of mobilising
the more or less willing in their villages, and required that
plans should be concerted for the selection of targets and the
fixing of times, but they did not require an elaborate or
permanent organisation and could be planned on an ad hoc
basis. The authoritative individual in the village community
would retain his sway, know his confederates, and stage his
local attacks between times, but there is no evidence to suggest
and no good reason to believe that he was in continuous
association with the like-minded elsewhere in some regularly
functioning system which controlled all operations. At the end
of the year, when the Yorkshire magistrates were rounding
up the persistent gangs of thieves who followed in the train of
Luddism, they were given information about Luddite organisation on the basis of units of ten, with a head man in charge
of a particular unit. These confessions relate particularly to
the way in which robber gangs were organised, but it is

Page 117: (*above*) Shears' Inn, Halifax Road, Hightown, much changed from the time when the Spen Valley croppers held their meetings there; (*below*) Westhoughton Mill, in the course of its lawful and successful demolition by contractors in 1899

Spencer Perceval Esqr Shirewood Camp. Decr 22 1811

Sir

The first & most important part of my Duty is to inform you & I request you do the same to all Colleagues in Office, also the Regent; that in consequence of the great sufferings of the Poor &c whose grievances seem not to be taken into the least consideration, by Government. I shall be under the necessity of again calling into action (not to destroy, many more frames)Ie. but — — — — — — — — — — my brave Sons of Shirewood, who are determin'd & sworn to be true & faithful avengers of their & Countrys wrongs. I have waited patiently to see if any measures were likely to be adopted by Parliamt. to alleviate distress in any shape whatever; but that hand of conciliation is shut & my poor suffering Country is left without a ray of hope: The Bill for Punishg. with Death. has only to be view'd with contempt & despis'd by measures equally strong: & the Gentlemen who fram'd it will have to Repent the act: for if one Mans life is Sacrificed. Blood for Blood. Should you be call'd upon you can't say I have not given you notice of it —

I have the honor to be
Genl E Ludd

possible that ten men had previously been thought a reasonable unit for a limited local Luddite attack and that such units helped the regimentation of the larger forces which were brought together for the bigger attack.[15]

Luddism in Nottinghamshire and the neighbouring counties seems not to have provoked the same belief that it was a highly institutionalised development based on a complex network of interrelated bodies. The Ned Ludd myth was stronger in Nottinghamshire than anywhere else in the country, and belief in it presupposed some tight central control exercised by a single powerful figure at the top, but such central control was neither likely nor necessary in the hosiery industry. The enormous number of successful raids carried out in Nottinghamshire over a very wide area, the proliferation of attacks in areas far apart on the same night, and the very detailed and precise knowledge necessary for the identification of offensive employers and offensive machinery, ensured that, while Midlands Luddism was widespread in late 1811 and early 1812, it must have been decentralised in its organisation. William Felkin believed that in this period there were four main companies of frame-breakers in the four centres of Sutton-in-Ashfield, Nottingham, Arnold, and Swanwick. Although there is no suggestion that they integrated their plans and organisation, the individual gangs seem to have established for themselves some primitive machinery for the raising of money from their fellow-workmen and to have been so tightly knit that their secrets could not be penetrated. Yorkshire Luddism died out in part because the magistrates arrested its main participants, but there was no such major triumph for the Nottinghamshire officials, and the so-called secrets of Luddite organisation there have remained secrets. The minor revival of frame-breaking in December 1812 and January 1813, mainly in Nottingham itself or very close by, was probably the work of only one gang. The last great phase of 1816 again seems largely the work of one body, this time of professional toughs, which was not necessarily constant in its composition but had a hard core of leaders such as Jem Towle, eventually hanged for the Loughborough job of June

H

1816, and his friends and relations who were allegedly anxious to demonstrate after Towle's removal that they could manage to do jobs without him.[16]

It is at this local level that the question of Luddite leadership has to be tackled, for it was, according to one account, 'the most daring and aspiring in each area' who became the General Ludd or leader. A single General Ludd there was none, though hopeful magistrates occasionally thought they had caught him, and even Peel later thought it 'not at all improbable' that 'the youth Ludlam actually directed secret bands', betraying some weakness in his historiography. For some Jem Towle was General Ludd, for others George Mellor, and the general himself, like Captain Swing his successor, remained only an idea embodying certain ideals. While Maitland was still floundering, he wrote on 6 May that it was very doubtful whether the principal Luddites in the area were themselves aware of the identity of those at the head of the system; they were aware of their own insignificance, he said, and so went to utmost lengths to push their cause by mentioning big names in association with it. Maitland evidently felt at this point that there was a system and that it had a head; earlier General Grey had made the popular upper-middle-class assumption that the systematic proceedings of the Luddites gave clear indication that their directors were persons 'above the common order of people, both in consequence and ability'. The idea died hard, but the Lords and the Commons were accepting by early July that the leaders were 'of the lowest Orders' and that the big names were dropped only to add apparent authority to what was being done by the Luddites. Neither the confessions of a dying rioter that he and his fellows were set on by a committee in London who regularly furnished them with money, nor the prison gossip about instructions which the London committee was about to send to all committees throughout the country to begin a general uprising, could obscure the fact that Luddism was purely a working-class movement, without patronage from higher social orders, and that its leaders emerged because of their own personal qualities, not their social or political eminence. It was quite a relief to the *Leeds Mercury* to be assured, in consequence of the York Assizes of January 1813, that not one person had been involved above the rank of those executed.[17]

If there was no great national figure to give cohesion and a unifying purpose to the activities of the Luddites, and if their local organisations were of a more informal kind than many contemporaries supposed, it must be asked what becomes of the national organisation and inter-district co-operation which many supposed to exist, and some still suppose to have existed. Did this really exist or was the Luddism of the North rather a copying of tactics pursued elsewhere, with nothing in common with the Midlands save a similar sort of response to the problems that faced working men? The most obvious link that needs to be established and proved to have existed in the Luddite chain is that between Nottinghamshire, the first centre of Luddite disturbance, and Yorkshire, the second main centre; yet evidence on this point, allegations even, seem almost non-existent. On 15 January George Coldham, the town clerk of Nottingham, wrote to the Mayor of Leicester that some of the Nottinghamshire frame-breakers were believed to be travelling into Leicestershire for the purpose of 'exciting the same spirit' which prevailed in their own area, and there is nothing inherently improbable in his suggestion. Whether or not the framework-knitters of Leicestershire needed the men of Nottinghamshire to make them aware of their grievances and to show them the way to tackle them, it would be according to trade practice for representatives of the Notts branches to travel the short distance involved to make contact with fellow-workmen inside different branches of the same industry. This is reasonable and acceptable. On 29 February, however, the Duke of Newcastle informed the Home Secretary that delegates from Nottingham were believed to be present in all the great towns in the country; this is unreasonable and unacceptable.

It is well known that at this time Gravener Henson was waging a campaign from Nottingham to secure parliamentary

regulation for the hosiery and lace trades, and that by dint
of enormous energy and enterprise he succeeded in making
contact, occasionally physically, with all the principal hosiery
and lace areas in Britain, including Ireland. It seems probable
that the few Nottingham leaders who were attempting to
link the hosiery areas were those to whom Newcastle referred,
but the reference was confused and contained a hopeless exaggeration. Furthermore, Newcastle also reported that the
disturbances which had recently taken place in Leeds had
been planned from Nottingham. This was a preposterous
notion; the Leeds episodes make perfect sense inside the context of the local woollen-cloth trade, and strangers from an
outside industry and from a distance of seventy miles would
not have possessed the specialised, local knowledge or control
to stage the events that did occur.

Other hints of a Nottinghamshire tie-up with Yorkshire are
equally unsatisfactory. R. A. Fletcher reported to the Home
Secretary on 21 January 1812 that Nottingham delegates were
present there, but this information he derived from the
apparently ubiquitous, omniscient Bent, who is admitted to
have been at his most unreliable when reporting on events
from which he was several stages removed. Another York-
shire/Nottinghamshire tie-up is suggested by Peel's fictionalised
account of Weightman's supposed visit to Halifax; this con-
tains enough inaccuracies to render it unacceptable, but it does
not, in any case, place Weightman's alleged visit until after the
establishment of the Luddite conspiracy in Yorkshire, with
Peel taking the line commonly followed at the time that the
Yorkshire croppers derived inspiration from reading about
Nottinghamshire Luddism in the press.[18]

Contemporary allegations concerning the spread of Luddism from Nottinghamshire are mostly that Midlands delegates were to be found in Lancashire, not Yorkshire. This
is strange in that Yorkshire Luddism, with its precise industrial programme, had much more in common with Nottinghamshire Luddism than did that of Lancashire; also it was
next in sequence. Lancashire might have been a more likely

place to evangelise than Yorkshire if a radical political campaign were being mounted, yet Nottinghamshire Luddism was purely industrial in its aims, certainly at the early stage when contacts were being alleged with Lancashire, and if political aims were being pursued the presence of Lancashire delegates in Nottinghamshire would have made more sense, and these were never reported. When Conant and Baker, the London police officers, investigated this problem in early February, they found nothing to tie up events in Nottingham with any other place or any outside organisation. The garbled letter of 17 April, sent from Dobcross post office in Yorkshire to relatives in Nottingham, which came into the possession of Joseph Radcliffe, looks like nothing more than a private communication between Luddite sympathisers and cannot be taken as evidence of any Luddite links between the two areas.[19]

It would seem that the reports of Nottingham men seen in Lancashire were either pieces of fiction, for they came from magistrates who freely employed spies and showed little if any discrimination in sifting their evidence, or that the men's presence had an explanation other than the magisterial one. The story retailed by W. Hay of the Manchester police office on 1 July, that three of Ludd's men had come from Nottingham, that they rode grey horses, that they came to give orders, and then rode off immediately, was probably fictitious. These were the only horse-riding Luddites to appear in the Luddite saga; what orders they came to give, why Manchester should take their orders, and why they rode off immediately after an already long ride were not explained. Similarly, the report on 23 March that Nottingham delegates were in Bolton, making converts and administering oaths to them, sounds highly improbable. There is no evidence that the Nottinghamshire Luddites were oath-takers or oath-administrators, and to what they were converting the people of Bolton is difficult to imagine. There is nothing in the history of Nottinghamshire Luddism to suggest that its interests could be served by sending representatives to other parts of the country to foment trouble of either an industrial or a political kind; the Nottinghamshire

Luddites belonged to the hosiery and lace trades and could not further their own ends by operating outside this context. There were reports from Stockport in December 1811 and January 1812 that delegates from Nottingham had met representatives of the weavers there; this might have been the case, though it is difficult to imagine who delegated them and for what purpose, since the framework-knitters did not begin to organise their parliamentary campaign until February 1812, and even then had no particular interest in making contact or common cause with men outside their own industry.

There were more delegates, this time from Carlisle and Glasgow as well as Nottingham, reported from Manchester on 11 February; they were said to be holding private meetings every night, but with whom and for what purpose was not clear. Nottingham, Manchester, Carlisle and Glasgow were, of course, the supposed route by which rebellion was being organised from London throughout Britain, but again it is not possible to find Nottinghamshire stockingers so employed inside their own community; they were all apparently needing to travel to secure appropriate recognition. On the same day, 11 February, subscriptions were allegedly being solicited in Stockport on behalf of the Luddites due to stand trial at the Nottinghamshire Spring Assizes. This sounds more feasible; who precisely was doing the soliciting, with that degree of success, and what was the ultimate destination of the money collected are all matters for speculation, but the presence of men engaged in something so practical and clearly stated sounds not improbable; it does not, of course, suggest a conspiratorial tie-up between Nottingham and Stockport, unlike the reports that R. A. Fletcher continued to receive and to believe. One such report was that Nottingham was in correspondence with Ireland, Scotland, and most parts of England, again a likely confusion with and distortion of Henson's organisation for the parliamentary campaign. Fletcher's informer had on this occasion rhetorically demanded of him if he thought the people of Nottingham (the Luddites presumably) would have subsisted so long if not supplied and supported by many well-wishers throughout the rest of Great Britain. Fletcher would doubtless have answered this question in the negative, but all evidence suggests that he would have been wrong to hold this opinion. And the wildness of half the informer's allegation is clearly a good reason for treating with scepticism the other half.

That there were people who regarded themselves as delegates and moved about Lancashire and parts of Cheshire is not questioned, though their importance is queried. That there were people who maintained regular and meaningful contact between Luddite organisations in Nottinghamshire and Lancashire is, however, strongly doubted. If it is allowed that the Nottinghamshire Luddites had no political designs, and no one who enquired into the matter thought they had, there really seems to be no reason why they should endeavour to make contacts inside the Lancashire cotton trade. Their protest movement was relevant only to their own trades; imitation of their conduct by outsiders could be of no possible assistance to them. Nottinghamshire, the first and main centre of Luddism, in terms of number of attacks, area covered, and duration of the crisis cannot be shown to have had contacts with Luddites and Luddism elsewhere; nor can any reason be shown why there should have been such contacts. It might have happened that 'the Luddites of different districts reached out to each other', but this they did spiritually; it is not possible to show that they did so physically, and it is even possible for someone 'who knows the geography of the Midlands and the North' to believe that the Nottinghamshire, or at least, the Midlands Luddites were essentially a self-contained body of people who neither had, nor needed, contact with those in the North.[20]

As far as links between the Luddites of Yorkshire and Lancashire are concerned, it is again a little difficult to see what either party had to gain by this unless a military rising were being planned; interests were separate, not complementary, and there were no joint attacks or demonstrations staged. Yarwood made references to Yorkshire delegates who produced several pounds at a certain trade meeting in Failsworth. This was one of the vaguest remarks in his entire confession, failing to identify the men, their origin, their purpose, or where they got their money, and equalling his account of the intention of 'opening connexions in London'. Even the Yorkshire/Lancashire tie-up, which was physically much more manageable in view of the short distance involved when compared with the distance both areas were from hosiery country, seems to depend on the reports of spies and the enthusiastic confessions of informers, rushing to unburden themselves and be of service, that there were 'committees' in all the manufacturing towns of the country, that they were in frequent communication with each other and constituted a 'system of confederacy', and that this complex network was somehow the supporter of Luddite outbreaks in Nottinghamshire, Derbyshire, Leicestershire, Yorkshire, Cheshire and Lancashire.[21]

The prevalence and extent of oath-taking are further matters in question. It was claimed in some quarters that illegal oaths were 'almost universal amongst the manufacturing and lower classes', oaths which, according to prison gossip, were being administered by men who were going about the country to perform the job at a wage of twenty shillings a week. The supposed oath, even when spelled out very clearly in its form, tended to remain somewhat vague in its purpose, being intended to bind together a fraternity engaged in secret and subversive behaviour which might be that of machine-breaking, political agitation, or even political revolution. Discussions of oath-taking were strongest when machine-breaking was least clearly to be seen as part of working-class industrial agitation, as in Lancashire, and they were most rarely heard where machine-breaking was most clearly to be seen. This is not to deny that secret oaths were administered and taken in 1812, but to suggest that the issue is marginal to a discussion of Luddism and that machine-breaking could be, and was, effectively carried out without a system of secret oaths.[22]

The evidence on the location and extent of oath-taking is, as on other allied subjects, confused. The Home Office, in its saner moments, found no reason to believe in oath-taking before March 1812 and the extension of Luddism to the North of England. In its less sane or more calculating moments, it was allowing the preparation of state briefs which recognised the existence of delegates from Nottingham who travelled to Bolton to administer oaths to 'persons rife for the purpose', and gave weight to the fact that the spy and provocateur Stones reported that John Becket had told him that he had received the oath from the Nottingham delegates. R. A. Fletcher certainly conveyed this information to the authorities in London, who rejected it when preparing their own summary of events but accepted it when preparing to indict prisoners. Both the sanctions that a local community could employ against the individual who betrayed the cause, and knowledge of how these were in fact invoked against particular individuals, create a supposition that Luddite secrets could be preserved in the hosiery and cropping communities without the need for a blood-curdling oath and in spite of the financial incentives offered by the authorities. And where betrayals did occur, it was the sanction of the community rather than that of the oath that was in fact invoked.[23]

The strongest rumour of oath-taking came from south Lancashire, and it was here that men came forward to take advantage of the Prince Regent's indulgence later. If this is to be considered a more probable area for oath-taking than the rest, it is because here machine-breaking was but one part of a very confused protest movement in which a few individuals might conceivably have seen themselves as leaders of some future revolution, and here that spies and provocateurs were most active, pushing people who started off as trade-union militants into indiscretions which made their behaviour treasonable. Yet here too the evidence is unsatisfactory and relies in part on stories of the stranger who first came to Dean Moor to administer illegal oaths and then escaped, along with another who came from London by coach 'to give directions', or the other 'strangers' supposedly responsible for 'twisting-in' considerable numbers in the Manchester area. The Dean Moor convictions for administering oaths are totally unsatisfactory evidence for their actual existence, though the continued certainty of General Maitland, as late as February 1813, that 'swearing-in' had featured prominently in Lancashire and Cheshire carries some weight. Yarwood might have been correct to allege that a 'twisting-in' system was being carried on rapidly by Buckley and two others amongst spinners and tailors, who were evidently being encouraged to believe that they were becoming part of some brotherhood that would effect changes; but the vague aspirations of some leaders and those who might have been persuaded to enlist behind them, if for no clear purpose, are no reason for supposing that the breaking of steam-looms, hardly a problem for spinners and tailors, was the outcome of an oath-bound conspiracy amongst handloom weavers, who achieved their objects by popular riots rather than by private conspiracy.[24]

A rather tortuous explanation has been offered of the alleged incidence of oath-taking in Yorkshire and Lancashire and its absence in Nottinghamshire. When Luddism spread to the North, it is suggested, machine-breaking meant death and the sanction of the oath was required to bind the conspirators closely to each other (in fact Yorkshire Luddism began in January and the new legislation came in February). And when the non-oath-taking Midlanders took up Luddism again in 1814 they persisted in refraining from oath-taking because this would have involved an additional capital offence. They were apparently willing to risk exposure to capital crime without the oath, which their northern colleagues were not prepared to do, and they were evidently deterred by the threat of capital punishment for oath-taking but not for frame-breaking.[25]

The role of spies in the promotion and organisation of Luddism also requires some consideration. In Nottinghamshire the town clerk, George Coldham, made repeated attempts to find informers who would supply him with Luddite secrets, or spies whom he could infiltrate into the ranks of the machine-breakers, but without success. Midlands Luddism was not in any sense the result of deliberately promoted unrest brought about at the instigation of the authorities. A somewhat extravagant suggestion has been made that in 1814 some hosiery firms deliberately attempted to provoke frame-breaking to give them a pretext for acting against the existing union society, but no evidence is advanced to support this view, which seems unlikely to be correct. The hosiers needed no such pretext; the union was already outside the law in spite of precautions taken to ensure its legality, and it collapsed after the Combination Laws, not the more recent legislation making frame-breaking a capital offence, had been invoked against three of its members. In Yorkshire and Lancashire, too, magistrates used whatever means they could for the detection of Luddism, and this included the shady operations of Nadin's disreputable characters, McDonald and Gosling, in Halifax, and the attempted introduction of clothworkers from the Wiltshire area into Luddite ranks, but there is no suggestion that Luddite activities in Yorkshire were anything other than working-class inspired and organised enterprises.[26]

As with so many aspects of Luddism, Lancashire is the exceptional area. Having a long tradition of magisterial readiness to employ spies and a few well-established professionals who profited from this readiness, it was an obvious field for provocateur activity once Luddism began. A classic statement on the attitude of R. A. Fletcher was given when he wrote, on 6 April, that he believed it proper to allow 'the Traitors' to proceed as far as possible without the commission of actual mischief in order that a greater number might be apprehended and more knowledge obtained of the 'first-movers'. He followed this with a statement of Luddite intention to fire Westhoughton the following Thursday. Now the 'first-mover' in the Westhoughton conspiracy was clearly John Stones, the spy in the employment of Fletcher. The depositions of men arrested after Dean Moor make it absolutely clear that they regarded Stones as their leader; he it was who organised the Luddites at Bolton, drilled them, filled their minds with tales of mythical Luddite organisation and plans elsewhere, threatened them if they failed to turn up for parades and refused to participate in the Westhoughton attack. The Hammonds' account of the Stones role is well documented and indicates that Bolton Luddism was as much contrived as it was the product of working-class discontent. The irony was that in spite of the repeated attempts by Stones to arrange the firing of the Westhoughton factory and in spite of the close contact between Stones and Fletcher, the attempts fell down and it was left to one of Lancashire's popular eruptions to do the job which Stones failed to do, at a time when Fletcher was away from home and local authorities were in a state of confusion and unpreparedness. In the light of this, it was nothing less than idiotic for Fletcher to report on 22 April, as an authoritative statement, that 'our confidential men have assured us that it was set on Fire by the Seditious and that this settled plan is by Fire in Secret to distract the Peace of the Country'. Stones was evidently salvaging what he could of his reputation, but his was a record of failure; he never got his Luddites to the scene of their intended crime, and when others arrived there he could not assist his employers in stopping them. Fletcher, too, was doubtless concerned to salvage his reputation, for it was hardly to his credit that Westhoughton should be destroyed by his enemies when he had been so fully in the picture for so long. The other cases of Luddism in the cotton industry pose no problems of spy involvement; the role of spies elsewhere was in part to inform on, and even develop, the notion of a general rising, and to assist in the detection and apprehension of the various categories of alleged criminals. There seems no reason for supposing that the Stockport attacks or the Middleton affair were in any way promoted by the activities of provocateurs.[27]

Nor does there appear to be any good reason for believing that the Luddites had the backing of some great exchequer which financed their multifarious activities. As late as 30 June 1812 the credulous Fletcher was still believing in the existence of 'a secret Fund supplied by aid from Quarters yet undiscovered', a fund, which, according to another source, stood at £40,000. It was this fund, presumably, from which all Luddites were getting an alleged 18s (90p) a week on being 'twisted-in'; according to another informant the 18s was for raw recruits and 21s (£1.5) was paid to 'those disciplined', but these sums went only to full-time Luddites who were otherwise out of work. The alleged 150 members of the Huddersfield gang were said, by Barrowclough, to get 14s (70p) a week, though they had the professional-class distinction of being paid monthly, and this same sum of money was elsewhere cited as the wage of those who were employed full-time in the administering of oaths. These tales were on the whole not taken seriously; the Home Office felt that accounts received of money supposedly paid out in connection with Luddism were either groundless or extremely exaggerated, and the House of Commons Committee of Secrecy could find no evidence of money having been distributed among the rioters. Machine-breaking, particularly with stolen implements, was not a costly operation to stage, and there was no need for large sums of money to be involved, except where it became a job for professionals as seems to have happened later in Nottinghamshire. Small subscriptions were probably exacted in parts of the hosiery area from a fairly early stage when frame-breaking appears to have been by the unemployed, supported in part by those in employment. Equally credible is Yarwood's account of the attempts to collect 1d or 2d per week from workmen in the Manchester area and the failure to total more than £5 or £6 to support a workers' union there. Accused men might merit collections amongst the sympathetic, and the Rawfold wounded might well have received the alleged collection of £10 6s 6d (£10.32½) on their behalf, but the world of Luddism was the world of petty rather than high finance, and money could never have played any important part in its organisation or sustenance outside Nottinghamshire, where it almost certainly did prolong Luddism's natural life.[28]

A last question on the organisation of Luddism which historians have asked repeatedly without necessarily answering satisfactorily is that concerning the extent to which it was supported and carried on through the more official and orthodox machinery of trade unionism. Part of the problem here is that trade unionism was itself proscribed in theory, however clearly it might have existed in fact, and so there is no clear distinction to be drawn between the legal and the illegal, the official and the unofficial aspects of labour organisation. Almost everything done by workmen to attempt to ameliorate their position was illegal, and machine-breaking was only one more illegal effort, if rather more dramatic than others. Nevertheless, with all this inevitable blurring of boundaries, it is still possible to recognise a labour approach that was concerned with the establishment of negotiating machinery or the use of constitutional forms and procedures, such as the parliamentary petitions, and these techniques betoken an approach quite different from that of industrial sabotage and direct action. It is often asked whether the two approaches were the work of different sets of people or whether they were the work of the same people at different times, whether Luddism was an extreme technique to which the trade unionist descended as a last resort or whether it was the method of the extremist who had never sought to solve workmen's problems in a more orthodox way. It is not possible to give to the questions a simple answer which is adequate for all areas of Luddism.

General Maitland's view of the Lancashire situation was that it had its origin in the efforts made by associations to keep up wages in the manufacturing trades. Finding 'their effort for this unavailing, they, in a moment of irritation, for which they had considerable grounds from the real state of distress in which they were placed, began to think of effecting their purpose by force'. Maitland was committed to the 'evolutionary' view of Luddism as a new technique by the old campaigners; the inside accounts of both Whittaker and Yarwood support this interpretation, though they do not confirm that Lancashire was in any sense a stronghold of a nationwide weavers' union at this time. Thomas Whittaker told how he was first associated with his fellow-workmen in attempts to raise wages by 'all legal means'; he was a delegate throughout

the cotton area, but his efforts and those of others proved unavailing. Eventually 'things began to wear a more serious
aspect' and secret committees began to be formed which
directed their attention to the destruction of machinery. In
the cotton areas, then, Luddism came in as a trade-union
technique when wage negotiations proved abortive, however
unrelated it may seem to the issue of wage negotiations. In
practice, however, though trade-union-type organisation might
have wanted to destroy steam-looms and might have been responsible for successfully staging a few minor outrages in
Stockport, the great acts of Lancashire Luddism, Middleton
and Westhoughton, owed most to popular commotion, accident and provocateurs, and apparently nothing to trade
unionism.[29]

It is even clearer in Yorkshire that the croppers, with their
small numbers and relatively high degree of organisation, had
not hesitated either to destroy or to threaten to destroy offensive
machinery for many years. As a prosperous group inside the
clothing trade, they had been able to turn their attention to
matters other than wages, matters such as preventing the introduction of the offensive gig-mills and shearing-frames, a central
plank in cropper trade-union orthodoxy; not for the croppers
any inhibitions about identification of themselves with violent
or reactionary policies. There would appear to be a direct
link between the Luddism of 1812 and earlier trade-union
history in the industry; in fact the events of 1812 suggest a
somewhat different view of the connection between Luddism
and trade unionism, namely that where trade unionism was
strong enough it could effectively achieve its aims without
resort to violence. In consequence, in the town of Leeds,
where the croppers were particularly well-organised and their
employers particularly overawed at the strength of the opposition, offensive machinery was kept out and Leeds hardly
featured in the Luddite story of 1812. The converse of this
was that where the croppers were more scattered, less well-
organised and weaker, the masters were stronger and readier
to introduce innovations, and Luddism resulted. And it

occurred not through established trade-union machinery but in its absence, deriving its strength from the small units of the scattered workshops which themselves, rather than any trade union, provided the basis for Luddite organisation.

In Nottinghamshire the situation is infinitely more complicated. There was no such thing as a union of the hosiery workers, but from time to time ad hoc organisations of varying sizes, covering different areas, would come into being to do a particular job, usually to negotiate a wage agreement, and then disappear. There was no background of existing formal trade-union organisation into which Luddism could fit when it appeared in 1811, though representatives of the men had tried abortively to prevent wage reductions before Luddism itself started. Luddism occurred, as in Lancashire, when more conventional methods had broken down, but it differed from the Lancashire version in two important respects. It was still the continuation of negotiations for the same ends but with other means, but it was a spontaneous eruption, in its early stages, and had to contend with the opposition of the usual leaders of the workmen throughout 1812. In February of that year Gravener Henson and a few fellow-workmen in the hosiery and lace trades began the ambitious and well-organised national petition to Parliament for the regulation of the two industries. Luddite methods were roundly condemned, though the Duke of Newcastle managed to confuse the two movements in spite of being personally visited by one of the petition organisers, Thomas Large, who was anxious to secure the Duke's patronage for the effort.[30]

The Nottinghamshire debate now centres on the role played throughout these affairs by Gravener Henson, the outstanding trade-union leader of the period and the dominant local figure for a quarter of a century. It is argued on the one hand that Henson remained totally aloof from and critical of the Luddites; and on the other hand that Luddism was an alternative or supplement to the usual, more constitutional techniques of the framework-knitters and that Henson probably oscillated between the two approaches. The principal grounds for believ-

Mr Wymnus

late foreman of a jury held
at nottingham 16 march - 12

Sir

by General Ludds Epress Epress

Commands I am come to —
Worksop to enquire of your Character
towards our cause and I am sorry
to say —I find it to correspond with
your conduct you latly shewed —
towards us, Remember the
time is fast aproaching When
men of your stamp Will be —
brought to Repentance, you may
be called upon soon. Remember —
you are a marked man

your for Genl Ludd
a true man

Page 135: Letter from General Ludd to the foreman of a Nottingham jury

This Paper was posted up in Nottingham on Saturday Morning
May 9th 1812

Welcome Ned Ludd, your case is good,
Make Perseval your aim;
For by this Bill, 'tis understood
It's death to break a Frame ——

With dexterous skill, the Hosiers kill
For they are quite as bad;
And die you must, by the late Bill —
Go on my bonny lad! ——

You might as well be hung for death
As breaking a machine ——
So now my Lad, your sword unsheath
And make it sharp and keen ——

We are ready now your cause to join
Whenever you may call;
So make foul blood run clear & fine
Of Tyrants great and small!. ——

with the Thomas   P.S. — Deface this who dare
Perceval Coaches   They shall have Tyrants fare
Ward Street   Forked is every where
                           And can see and hear ——

Page 136: A poem in praise of Ned Ludd

ing that Henson remained untainted by Luddism are that he himself said so, that he and his colleagues repeatedly condemned Luddism during their 1812 campaign to secure parliamentary regulation of the trade, and that the methods of the Luddites were so alien to a man of Henson's methods and persuasions. These grounds seem rather slight. Henson was unlikely to admit himself guilty of capital offences, either at the time or later when he was appearing before parliamentary commissions or mingling with cabinet ministers. The official condemnation of Luddism during the first half of 1812 proves only that Luddism was regarded as tactically mistaken while Henson was trying to further the workmen's ends by other means; his political persuasions made him an unacceptable ally of the Nottingham Whigs and open to suspicion of insurrectionary conspiracy, and a preference for constitutional methods is no proof of a willingness to employ others if the occasion demanded it. There was undoubtedly a great weight of suspicion and mistrust of Henson, who was widely believed to be involved in Luddism, though it must be admitted that the case cannot be proved either way.

It is possible that the Luddite outbursts in the spring of 1811 suggested alternative means to the trade unionists, who gave some direction to frame-breaking in the latter part of that year. It is certain that frame-breaking largely died away during the appeal to Parliament in 1812 and that such as continued was an embarrassment to the trade unionists. It seems likely however, that when frame-breaking reappeared in 1814, it was being used selectively against particular employers to supplement by coercion the more orthodox methods of the union society to secure wage increases for its members. The occasions of its employment tie in so closely with the society's own campaigns that it becomes difficult to dissociate the two. When the trade union collapsed after the invoking of the Combination Acts in July 1814, frame-breaking appeared to lose its direction and degenerated into general plunders and disorder. During its final phase in 1816 the gangster-like element was again strong, but there was widespread belief that the gangs were

I

working to orders which came from quasi-unions. Lace-frames especially were under fire at this stage, and informal committees of warp-lace and bobbin-net workers were believed to be responsible for attacks which included that on Heathcoat's Loughborough factory, where the question of wages was particularly at issue.[31]

In general it can be said of Midlands Luddism, and of that in Yorkshire too, that whatever the precise involvement of trade-union personnel and machinery, Luddism did arise as a supplement to other trade-union techniques. Had these been sufficient to achieve the aims of the workmen, there would have been no Luddism. It is less easy to apply this generalisation to Lancashire, since machine-breaking, although in part a last resort for frustrated trade unionists, was also an outlet for popular violence which had many causes and little precise direction.

1   *Nottingham Review*, 15 March 1811; *Nottingham Journal*, 16 March 1811; Sutton, J. F. *The Date Book of Nottingham* pp 291-4

2   Darvall, F. O. *Popular Disturbances and Public Order* . . . . p 88; HO 40/10, Blackburn's confession, 9 January 1817; Sutton, J. F. *The Date Book of Nottingham* p 334; Felkin, W. *History of the Machine Wrought Hosiery* . . . . p 240

3   *Leeds Mercury*, 18, 25 January, 29 February 1812; HO 42/122, Foster to HO, 20 April 1812; Peel, F. *The Risings of the Luddites* p 41; Thompson, E. P. *The Making* . . . . p 577

4   eg Yarwood's Statement of 22 June 1812 in HO 40/1

5   HO 42/122, Foster to HO, 20 April 1812; *Leeds Intelligencer*, 13, 20 April 1812; HO 42/122, Cartwright to HO, 23 April 1812; Bailey to HO, 12 April 1812; Peel, F. p 40; TS 11/980, 3580; HO 40/1, Fletcher to HO, 22 April 1812; Depositions of prisoners in HO 42/128; HO 40/1, Lloyd to HO, 17 June 1812

6   Report of House of Commons Committee of Secrecy, 8 July 1812; *Leeds Mercury*, 18 January, 29 February, 21, 28 March 1812; *Leeds Intelligencer*, 23 March 1812

7   Thompson, E. P. *The Making* . . . . pp 588, 568; *Manchester*

Mercury, 21 April 1812; *Leeds Mercury,* 22 August 1812; HO 42/122, W. Chippendale to HO, 21 April 1812

8 Peel, F. *The Risings of the Luddites,* pp 6, 15, 17, 24, 25; John Booth, an apprentice saddle and harness maker, killed at Rawfolds, was exceptional; Fitzwilliam MSS 46/127; HO 42/124, Précis of troubles in Northern Counties, June 1812

9 Thompson, E. P. *The Making* . . . . p 543

10 HO 42/123, Priestley to HO, 18 May 1812

11 HO 40/1, 'Ned Ludd' to Mr Smith, undated; HO 42/123, Précis of troubles, op cit; HO 42/122, Flixton to HO, 19 April 1812; *Leeds Mercury,* 9 May 1812; Fitzwilliam MSS 46/44; HO 42/126, Maitland to HO, 24 August 1812; HO 42/138, Maitland to HO, 18 February 1813; HO 42/129, Hobhouse to HO, 29 November 1812

12 HO 42/122, Manchester Police Office to HO, 22 April 1812; HO 42/123, Campbell to General Grey, 1 May 1812; HO 42/124, Précis of troubles

13 HO 42/125, Hardie to HO, 21 July 1812

14 HO 42/123, Maitland to HO, 6 May 1812

15 Peel, F. *Spen Valley Past and Present* p 240; HO 42/130, Confession of James Hay, 14 December 1812

16 Felkin, W. *History of the Machine Wrought Hosiery* . . . . p 231; Darvall, F. O. *Popular Disturbances and Public Order* . . . . p 157

17 Historical Account, p 7; Peel, F. *The Risings of the Luddites* p 12; 42/123, Maitland to HO, 6 May 1812; HO 42/121, Grey to HO, 25 March 1812; *Manchester Mercury,* 12 May 1812; HO 40/1, information of J. Johnson, 10, 12, 13 May 1812; *Leeds Mercury,* 23 January 1813

18 HO 42/119, Coldham to Mayor of Leicester, 15 January 1812; HO 42/120, Newcastle to HO, 29 February 1812; HO 42/119, Fletcher to HO, 21 January 1812; Peel, F. *The Risings of the Luddites* pp 26-7

19 HO 42/120, Conant and Baker to HO, 6 February 1812; Radcliffe MSS 126/32

20 HO 42/125, Hay to HO, 1 July 1812; HO 42/121, Fletcher to HO, 23 March 1812; HO 42/118, Bulkely to HO, 26 December 1811; HO 42/119, Bulkely to HO, 1 January 1812; HO 42/120, Kayer to HO, 11 February 1812; Ibid, Lloyd to HO, 11 February 1812; Ibid, Fletcher to HO 25 February 1812; Thompson, E. P. *The Making* . . . . pp 600, 577

21 HO 40/1, Yarwood's statement, 22 June 1812; HO 42/124, Précis of troubles

22 Raynes, F. *An Appeal to the Public* p 51; HO 40/1, informa-
    tion of J. Johnson, 10, 12, 13 May 1812
23 HO 42/124, Précis of troubles; TS 11/980, 3580; HO 42/121,
    Fletcher to HO, 23 March 1812; eg Hammond, J. L. and B.
    The Skilled Labourer p 269, describe how John and Elizabeth
    Braithwaite, who gave evidence to convict William Carnell
    and Joseph Maples at Nottingham, were forced to move to a
    distant part of the country for their own safety
24 HO 42/123, Lascelles to HO, 5 May 1812; HO 127, Faring-
    ton to HO, 13 September 1812; HO 42/132, Maitland to
    HO, 18 February 1813; HO 40/1, Yarwood's statement of
    22 June 1812
25 Thompson, E. P. *The Making* . . . . pp 577-8
26 Ibid p 573; Radcliffe MSS 126/10
27 HO 40/1, Fletcher to HO, 6, 22, 26 April; HO 42/132,
    deposition of prisoners; Hammond, J. L. and B. *The Skilled
    Labourer* pp 277-286
28 HO 42/124, Fletcher to HO, 30 June 1812; HO 40/1, undated
    address 'To all Croppers, Weavers etc, and the Public at
    Large'; *Leeds Intelligencer,* 6 July 1812; Fitzwilliam MSS
    45/135; HO 42/125, Barrowclough's deposition, 8 July 1812;
    HO 42/122, Flixton to HO, 19 April 1812; HO 42/124.
    Précis of troubles; HO 40/1, Yarwood's statement of 22 June
    1812; HO 42/129, Examination of John Bates, 5 November
    1812
29 HO 42/124, Précis of Maitland's communication from Man-
    chester, 22 June 1812; HO 42/123, Whittaker to the Governor
    of Chester Castle, undated; HO 40/1, Yarwood's statement of
    22 June 1812
30 Nottingham Borough Records, Framework-Knitters' Papers,
    1812-14; Newcastle MSS NeC 4, 920
31 See Church, R. A. and Chapman, S. D. 'Gravener Henson
    and the Making of the English Working Class' in *Land,
    Labour and Population in the Industrial Revolution* (1967) ed
    Jones and Mingay; Thompson, E. P. postscript to second
    edition of *The Making of the English Working Class* (1968)
    and Thomis, M. I. *Old Nottingham* (1968) Ch 12

Chapter Five

LUDDISM AND LAW AND ORDER

LUDDISM MEANT DIFFERENT things to different people. To those concerned with the processes of government, at central or local level, it was essentially a problem of law and order. It bears further examination as such, not simply because of points to be noted about technical questions of administration, the processes of detection and arrest, or the deployment of military forces, for instance, but also because of the further light to be thrown thereby on the nature of Luddism and the nature of the society in which it occurred.

In the first place any assessment of the nature of the threat posed by Luddism demands an accurate chronicling and recording of its events, so that it may be known whether the authorities of the day were faced with five, fifty, or five hundred episodes of machine-breaking. Yet an accurate statement of the events of Luddism is very difficult to come by. Just as contemporaries were inclined to overstate the size of the threat facing them, so have historians been inclined to exaggerate the number of incidents which occurred and the geographical breadth of area they covered. It might conceivably be considered a local historian's licence to identify local problems as national ones and to pretend that because a phenomenon was common to a number of Midland and Northern counties it in fact covered the whole country, but it behoves the national historian to bring more precision to the dating of the events and thereby to the judging of their intensity.

Yorkshire and Lancashire, though apparently experiencing so few episodes of machine-breaking as to leave little scope for disagreement about their number and dating, have nevertheless left problems. Baines, writing from and about cotton country, talked of 'riotous opposition to all new machines', which there certainly was not; he named the outstanding cases of Luddism and vaguely referred to 'other places' which experienced it, yet cases of Luddism in Lancashire can be counted on the fingers of one hand. Similarly, the Yorkshire episodes have been difficult to count. A recent description of 'nightly attacks' in Huddersfield and Spen Valley during the month of February 1812 could be justified only on the interpretation of 'nightly' as meaning 'at night'. There were in this period two 'nightly' attacks in Huddersfield and none in Spen Valley.

And just as Yorkshire's few have been multiplied, so have Nottinghamshire's many, and imaginations have run riot in their recording. The most serious period of Luddism in the hosiery industry occurred during the last two months of 1811 and the opening month of 1812. F. O. Darvall says, four times over, that during this period there were Luddite attacks every night; on a fifth occasion he states, rather more cautiously, that during this time hardly a night passed without at least one Luddite attack. In addition, he states that there were usually several attacks on one night. Now if 'usually' is interpreted as meaning only four times a week and 'several' as meaning 'three', there is strong implication of a weekly minimum of fifteen attacks, and a grand total of practically 200 attacks during this three-month period. In fact this conservative figure is about double the number of Luddite attacks which occurred. It is not true that attacks occurred every night or that there were usually several on one night. Weekends, especially Sunday nights, were particularly busy times, but there were many quiet nights in between. Darvall was not prone to exaggeration on points of detail, yet managed nevertheless to summarise events in highly colourful and misleading language, preparing the way for a later account to allege that Nottinghamshire Luddism 'continued without intermission until Feb-

ruary 1812 . . . Night after night, for more than three months
. . . sometimes in two or three widely separated villages on
the same night'. This is standard belief, but it is inaccurate
and misleading reporting. Perhaps it is no more misleading
than the contrast recently drawn between the so-called Luddism of 1826 in Lancashire and the 'sporadic and small-scale
frame-breaking of 1811-12'. Others might have overstated the
case, but this understatement is equally confusing.[1]

The tendency to exaggerate springs in part from the forming of an idealised view of Luddism, where the ideal is a
society continuously and seriously challenged by its working
class over a long period. It springs in part, too, from the conflicts and exaggerations inside the evidence itself. The Nottinghamshire which the outside world saw was not the Nottinghamshire of the county's residents. The *Leeds Mercury,* a
moderate, non-alarmist publication, produced a sensational
account of the death and funeral of John Westley, a Luddite
shot at Bulwell in November 1811, which it accompanied by
stories of other woundings in the various conflicts which had
allegedly taken place in the area. It gave no precise details of
the civil war which it seemed to be describing. By 21 December it reported that the insurrectional state of the county
had no parallel since the reign of Charles I, and six weeks later
produced a further instalment in the saga: the town of Nottingham was in a state of the greatest alarm, people were afraid
to go to bed as a general ransacking of the town had been
threatened, and General Ludd had declared his intention of
destroying all frames without exception. Now the curious
thing about Nottingham during the Luddite period is how
peaceful it remained, never becoming a town of panic and
disturbance. The point was clearly made by Conant and Baker
when they reported to the Home Office in February 1812.

Notwithstanding what was said in the Times newspaper, this place has been in the most perfect quiet ever
since we have been in it. Indeed we often observe that
we have never known any place approaching to the same

population, so wholly free from any species of disorder and particularly at night.

This was not the Nottingham which the press was describing to the world. Machine-breaking appears to have posed no threat and carried no fear to those not immediately concerned with it.[2]

It is not surprising, in view of this, that the more imaginative commentators of Nottinghamshire and elsewhere left erroneous accounts of the events they reported. The *Manchester Mercury,* following the attack upon Westhoughton, reported that many other factories and mills were due to meet the same fate, that the lives of many respectable people had been threatened, but that the Bolton militia had thrown these plans into disarray by a 'well-conceived project', seized the papers of the conspirators, a welcome supplement to Luddite evidence had they materialised, and arrested a number of ringleaders including a man known as General Ludd, 'the grand administrator of impious, rebellious, oaths'. Were this account to stand unsupplemented by those which unfold the sordid story of R. A. Fletcher and 'Old' and 'Young' Stones, father and son, Lancashire Luddism would indeed assume formidable proportions, and the plight of the authorities in coping with it would have been an extremely serious one.[3]

Luddite attacks were not so numerous as they seemed to be, nor was their menace so great as many contemporaries imagined. But that is not to deny the existence of a great fear and the fact that immense numbers of troops were involved in freeing society from it. It is a well-known and much-quoted point that the army of 12,000 required for domestic use to suppress the Luddites was a greater force than Wellington had taken to Portugal in 1808, though this must not be confused with the army of nearly 70,000 men with whom Wellington eventually fought Napoleon at Waterloo. The army against the Luddites might have been six times as large as any needed previously for domestic disputes, and the 1,800 soldiers used in Nottingham by late November 1811 a larger force than any previously used for a purely local disturbance, but there had not been any occasion for such an army previously. Luddism was something new, and so comparisons are not particularly helpful. There were civil wars, religious riots, food riots and industrial riots in the previous two centuries, but there had never been such wide-scale industrial riots occurring simultaneously with food riots in an industrial revolution context, where the problems of three major industries reached crisis point. And all this was happening during the greatest war that the country had ever waged, with an economy now dependent on overseas trade which could not be sustained. The 1,500 special constables of Salford or the 1,000 soldiers billeted in the thirty-three public houses of the small town of Huddersfield constituted numbers that these places had not previously experienced, but the problem too was unprecedented. The actual numbers tell us that the new phenomenon was frightening but not that it was dangerous to the point of constituting a threat to public order throughout the country, to society, or to government.[4]

Official reaction to Luddism at the highest level revealed a surprising sang-froid. The subject did not come before Parliament until February 1812 when the worst Nottinghamshire troubles were already over, and then it appeared to creep into the business of the House of Commons almost by accident. It occupied very little of the House's time during the coming months, and attracted only small audiences, hardly indicative of a country on the brink of revolution or social anarchy. There was new legislation to make frame-breaking and the administering and receiving of oaths capital offences and for more effectively ensuring the peace of Nottingham, the last of which was never fully implemented. It was the Home Office view that additional penal laws would enable magistrates to act more effectively, but there was no evidence to support this view and strong suggestion that it was an erroneous one. The *Leeds Mercury* was quick to point out that the detection of offenders was made no more easy by increasing penalties, and the Nottingham magistrates informed the Home Secretary that their task was now made that much harder, since all sources of information had dried up, people being unwilling to implicate offenders now that conviction meant death. General Maitland pressed for legislation to give magistrates the arbitrary power to conscript into the armed forces for a limited period 'persons of bad character'; mercifully his promptings were ignored, for many magistrates were clearly not to be trusted with such an offensive discretionary power. Nor did the government even grant them the power that a suspension of Habeas Corpus would have meant, which was at times requested.

Apart from the increasing of penalties for offences, an almost instinctive reaction and one largely irrelevant to the problem, there was little to suggest that the government felt itself faced with other than little local difficulties. It was important, wrote Treasury Solicitor Henry Hobhouse from Chester on 30 May, that someone should be executed for each of the three categories of crime with which the authorities were currently concerned: 'Robbers under colour of begging, Robbers under colour of purchasing, and Breakers of machinery.' It was important too, to convict Thomas Whittaker, because he was a man of superior ability and education and his crime was all the greater because of this. They did not need to punish all offenders; perhaps the guilt of the convicted was not of prime importance as long as the violated laws were upheld and sacrificial victims could be found as an example to the rest of society. Hobhouse seems to have embodied government attitudes and policies throughout; on 9 January 1813 he was reporting the favourable effect of the York executions on the local populace, and some days later he was instructing Joseph Radcliffe of Huddersfield that it was not Lord Sidmouth's wish that he should continue to track down Luddites with his former zeal. The law had been satisfied; there was no need to encourage further social antagonism beyond this point. It was 'of infinite importance to society' that no mercy should be shown to the convicted men, but it was not important to proliferate the convictions if the trouble had stopped, and it appeared to have stopped with the removal of the ringleaders. The government attitude might be described as pragmatic rather than ideologically based; with all its class prejudice and lack of humanity, the government was concerned to restore things to normal and to keep the engine ticking over rather than to prevent a revolution occurring in the future. The difficulty it had in doing this was determined by the machinery at its disposal rather than the size of the problem.[5]

The key figure in this situation was the local magistrate, and the success with which the problem of Luddism was tackled in any one area was determined by his energy, resolution and intelligence. Unfortunately the high qualities and initiative which the successful pursuit of Luddites demanded were not markedly present inside the magisterial group; it was distinguished by its incompetence and misjudgements rather than by qualities making for success. An exceptionally able and successful magistrate was Joseph Radcliffe of Milnsbridge, Huddersfield, who appears to have worked ceaselessly, tirelessly and fearlessly throughout 1812 and to have been personally responsible for the apprehension and conviction of the principal figures in Yorkshire Luddism. To the *Leeds Mercury*, which remained highly critical of the methods of his less savoury colleagues on the bench, he was 'that indefatigable and intrepid magistrate', and it was a well-earned baronetcy which Earl Fitzwilliam finally secured for him as a reward for his services. Radcliffe apart, the West Riding magistrates did not make a very impressive showing.

The Home Office found occasion to remind Fitzwilliam of the powers and obligations that attended his office and evidently felt no great confidence in his administration; it was believed, wrote Maitland on 16 May 1812, that the West Riding lieutenancy was not only giving no assistance to the government's plans but was actually paralysing every effort to get things organised. A month later the deputy-lieutenant, Sir Francis Wood, admitted having found the magistrates completely divided about measures to be adopted against the Luddites, and even in August Maitland still complained that they were having great difficulty in getting the magistrates and peace officers of the West Riding to act. In part their weakness was an inability to judge the situation accurately; in part it appears to have been a question of fear or even cowardice. Many of the Yorkshire magistrates 'have betrayed pusillanimity', wrote Richard Walker from Huddersfield to Fitzwilliam on 9 July; this showed itself particularly in the extravagant demands for protection that all were in the habit of making. Each thought his own area in the greatest danger of attack, wrote General Grey to the Home Secretary, and some wished for military guards in all towns; if he were to indulge them all, the entire army in England would be insufficient to meet the requirements of the West Riding alone. Nor were they apparently capable of distinguishing between the needs of their present situation and a sense of alarm which derived from outrages long since over.[6]

In Lancashire Maitland had found an equally discouraging situation. He wrote, mildly, on 4 May that the magistrates there were 'not acting with understanding among themselves'. Two days later he reported that there had been a meeting of the lieutenancy without any attempt to communicate with the officer commanding troops in the area, with resultant confusion, and asked that all magistrates should be instructed to communicate with him personally and directly. Instead of this, J. Lloyd, for instance, of Stockport, was proposing a jaunt to London to see the Home Secretary when he would have been better remaining at his post and passing on his information to Maitland. Another problem was the petty jealousies of the magistrates regarding the retention of local information for their own exploitation. Two years later Joseph Nadin, the deputy constable of Manchester, added further weight to the charges of failure to co-operate when he recalled his inability to secure a single constable from the townships around Manchester when the town itself was plagued with a multiplicity of mobs.

But perhaps worse than any of these weaknesses and faults were the intrigues into which a number of people entered, which went far to obscure the true situation in Lancashire and contributed little to its clarification. Nadin himself was an incurable intriguer and unscrupulous provocateur, as the case of the '38' clearly shows; the ramifications of his enterprises stretched as far as Halifax, where his agents were responsible for the case against Baines and the evidence on which he was convicted. Lloyd of Stockport appears a fanatic whose peripatetic efforts in pursuit of Luddites took him throughout the northern counties and involved him in most of the shady devices by which evidence was accumulated and men trapped. On 29 August he wrote from Yorkshire that he had 'prevailed over Hinchcliffe to identify Schofield': two days later he characterised his methods when he wrote that if he was ever to make anything out of witnesses 'it must be by suddenly taking them up and running away with them to a distance', kidnapping, as it was alternatively and more directly called elsewhere. But the most notorious case, because it produced such a fiasco, was that of R. A. Fletcher, who really does seem to have lived in a dream world of his own creation. Had Thistlewood succeeded in eliminating the Cabinet in 1820 it would have been the same sort of administrative blunder, though on a grander scale, as Fletcher's conspiracy to destroy Westhoughton mills, the destruction of which he was unable to prevent. It was men such as these, more dangerous in their excessive zeal than the Yorkshire officials in their apathy, with whom General Maitland had to work, and he admitted to finding the whole subject of intelligence one of great embarrassment and much more of a problem than he had expected. He appreciated the menace of the zealots just as he deprecated the inertia of the rest, but when faced with the task of advising on the question of a baronetcy for Radcliffe, the soundest of them all, he felt compelled to speak against the idea in case it should seem that the government was reduced to offering bribes in order to persuade magistrates to do their duty.[7]

The magistrates of Nottinghamshire seem to have lacked the taste for intrigue and the desire to make a career out of prosecuting Luddites which characterised some of their Lancashire colleagues. George Coldham and his successor, Henry Enfield, both attempted to play the espionage game in the hope of acquiring information, but this they did in the absence of any other method of making headway and they had in any case almost no success. By the time of Pentrich, in 1817, Enfield had built up a better service for himself, but his Luddite informants were little help. In spite of this the Nottingham magistrates won for themselves considerable praise and the reputation for administering their town very efficiently; this was contrasted with the alleged inefficiency and apathy of the magistrates of the country areas, for it was within the jurisdiction of the latter that the vast majority of machine-breaking cases occurred. In fact, despite their long-established rivalry with the county officials, the agents of the Whig Corporation's great foe, the Duke of Newcastle, the town magistrates assumed no air of superiority, realising fully that their own task was infinitely easier than that faced by their long-suffering county colleagues.[8]

If the local officers of the law constituted one of the most serious obstacles to its proper enforcement, the nature of the force to be employed against the Luddites was also a serious problem. A large army might be a realisable asset on a battlefield, but the campaigns of the Luddites represented anything but military orthodoxy and posed problems of strategy and tactics which were never properly resolved. On Maitland's arrival in Lancashire in early May, he soon expressed disapproval of the policy of dissipating resources by scattering tiny detachments of soldiers throughout a great number of towns and villages; his wish was to keep troops in a central position ready to give aid when it was required. This view, based on the principle that a 'multiplicity of small detachments is extremely to be avoided' derived in part from the Lancashire experience of a few very serious episodes, involving large numbers of people and therefore requiring large numbers of soldiers. Concentration for these occasions was desirable; it was also based on Maitland's belief that the army simply could not cater for the needs and supposed needs of every small town and village. It was a mistake to attempt to supply these places with enough soldiers for their own defence, since this relieved the locality from defending itself and made people lazy and apathetic. In the later stages of Lancashire Luddism, and in Yorkshire and Nottinghamshire, the policy rejected by Maitland made better sense. Here the army was not concerned with large pitched battles, but with a great number of small incidents which might better be tackled by having many small parties of soldiers moving about rapidly in patrols on missions of crime prevention and detection rather than for fighting pitched battles.[9]

In spite of the very large numbers of soldiers involved against Luddism, the army's record against the machine-breakers was not a successful one. So adept were the Nottinghamshire Luddites at dodging the military patrols that the *Leeds Mercury* was prompted to enquire whether this was a matter of deliberate neglect arising out of the army's commiserating with the lot of the men. In Yorkshire the Luddites had an unbroken run of successes until Rawfolds Mill, and even there they were repulsed by the determination of the mill-owner, a few faithful hands, and four or five soldiers who had been lent for the purpose—and one of these refused to fight against the attackers. Even the continuous tolling of the factory bell throughout the attack failed to summon military aid to the besieged, and it was not until the attackers had been dispersed that soldiers finally arrived, though they were quartered at public houses within a two-mile radius of Rawfolds, which had been an obvious target for Luddism for some time.

In the two great set-pieces of Lancashire Luddism, Middleton and Westhoughton, the former was successfully defended against the attackers by the owner's family and employees; the latter represented the grossest case of inefficiency and incompetence somewhere along the line. According to local press reports, West Houghton was guarded by soldiers until twelve noon, at which time they marched off; soon afterwards the job was done. Ralph Fletcher explained to the Home Office that after the force had been summoned to Westhoughton earlier, apparently on a wild-goose chase, Captain Buller had resolved not to move again except on the specific order of Mr. Sutton, a magistrate in the neighbourhood. This resolution contributed nothing to the army's record of achievement. Soldiers in a troubled area presented their own problems; they might get themselves involved in local brawls and in the opinion of such as the Duke of Newcastle were liable to be tampered with; he thought it of the utmost importance that they should be kept entirely separate from the local populace except when they were required for action. But in spite of this, and in spite of their record of failure, the regular soldiers were the favourites of the local magistrates, who had a strong preference for them as opposed to the militia forces they were entitled to command. In Yorkshire in particular, General Maitland was very annoyed to find that all the magistrates were demanding regular soldiers, and it was not until mid-May that he was able to report that 'we have got rid of their fancy for not employing local Militia'.[10]

The militia men had some very harsh things said about them during the Luddite outbreaks. By their very composition they were thought to be unreliable. Richard Hardy of Loughborough wrote that he was unable to persuade himself that they were at any time a force to be relied upon to suppress riot, especially if this arose out of the high price of provisions in a town where most of the men had friends and relations. According to Colonel Wroughton, writing from Wakefield, there was no confidence in the militia anywhere in the manufacturing districts; they were more likely to join rioters than to oppose them and in many instances men had joined the militia only to learn how to use weapons so that they could turn their knowledge to sinister purposes. There was a widespread view that the militia men could be effectively used only many miles away from their home base; in their own area they would join the insurgents, as the commanding officer of the Sheffield local militia alleged after the food riots there in mid-April, or they would form part of the local Luddite organisation, as Josiah

Foster of Horbury alleged after the attack on his father's mill, or they would be the means of running guns to the Luddites, as was suggested from Hipperholme, near Halifax. Even away from home they could have their minds poisoned by local inhabitants, as allegedly happened to the West Norfolk militia on duty in Loughborough, which fact they demonstrated by their mutinous conduct. At home they were among 'the most powerfully disaffected', and it was an article of Yorkshire faith that to arm and employ them was nothing but folly. The accusations and the reality were not necessarily close together. General Maitland, in his wish to keep pressure off his regular forces, was firm in the view that the militia was a necessary and reliable part of the forces of order; he gave little weight to the various assertions of disloyalty on the part of its members and maintained that in Lancashire, where it was widely employed, he had experienced no single case of impropriety in its behaviour.[11]

But the armed forces, whether regulars or militia, had their limitations, and it was these that Maitland was never able to get the local magistrates to recognise. Time and time again he reminded them that the army's job was to prevent insurrection and really serious threats to public order; it was not the army's job to provide guards for the private property of individuals. Maitland resented the army playing at policemen and deplored the readiness with which the localities assumed that it could be called in to solve all their problems. On his arrival in Lancashire he proclaimed his belief that it was up to the 'higher orders of the community' to adopt measures to protect their own property, as the model property-owner, William Cartwright, had done at Rawfolds. A combination of property, he wrote, is the only answer to a combination against property, and this was not emerging. The arrival of so many soldiers had weakened the exertions of local people, who were now applying for troops at the very slightest alarm. Apathy, fear, antagonism even, were widely encountered on both sides of the Pennines. Fitzwilliam received repeated reports of a disinclination to form associations against the

K

Luddites in the disturbed areas of the West Riding. The militant parson, Hammond Roberson, writing from within a good stone's throw of Rawfolds Mill on 30 April, lamented: 'There is not an inhabitant in all this neighbourhood that I know of that is at all alive to the situation of the country, or rather perhaps, that is able and that dares to take any decisive part in directing the operations of the military besides myself.'

Private associations of property were formed at Halifax and Huddersfield, but the problems of implementing watch and ward in the West Riding proved insuperable. It was resisted in part because of its expense, on the ground that high poor rates and high food prices made any further burden intolerable, and magistrates lacked the resolution or courage to push it through in face of the demonstrations of opposition; so much so that it was established in only two townships. When Colonel Campbell reported to General Grey on 1 May that he knew of nothing more that could be done than what had already, with Grey's sanction, been done, this was no complacency but a virtual admission of defeat.[12]

Employers were frequently taken to task for their failure to act together and with resolution against the Luddites. The Nottinghamshire hosiers were said to be spending their time abusing each other in public print when they should have been acting in concert against the frame-breakers. Eventually they formed their committee to prosecute frame-breakers and secured the co-operation of the town clerk, George Coldham, as secretary; but they never prosecuted any frame-breakers, only three offenders against the Combination Acts in July 1814, and were never able to present a united front on wages long enough to satisfy the framework-knitters. Similarly in Leeds, subscriptions were undertaken by merchants and manufacturers in late February 1812 to prosecute workmen guilty of combination, particularly regarding opposition to machinery, but the efforts of employers were thought to be feeble and they apparently made little contribution to the ending of Luddism.[13]

Perhaps the most serious handicap of all which the authorities suffered was the fact that machine-breaking was carried out against a background of considerable public sympathy for the plight of the workmen. Though this did not extend to actual approval of the methods of the Luddites, it did guarantee the law-breakers a large measure of protection against efforts at apprehension. Dilatory conduct on the part of those whose premises were invaded often suggested a measure of sympathy with the purposes of the Luddites that officials found most reprehensible. There was 'a shyness in speaking of the subject' which might have been partly a matter of fear but probably arose, too, from a desire not to turn the dogs loose on those who had been reduced to Luddism in an effort to solve their problems. It was active sympathy rather than 'apathy and torpor' which allowed the Fartown attackers a free hand in November 1812 before the authorities were notified of the trouble; and the ability of Nottinghamshire Luddites to be 'spirited away', having been almost caught in the act, or Yorkshire Luddites to be absorbed into a community which refused to disgorge them, can be explained only in terms of the public sympathy they received. If money failed to buy the disclosures of the working men from whom the Luddites came, there are also strong suggestions that the Luddites were not without sympathisers from other social groups. Peel believed that many of the middle and trading classes had sympathy for them, and this was supported by the Headingley correspondent who informed the Home Secretary on 15 April 1812 that even among the respectable part of the population there was popular support for the Luddites. One group of men which might have given considerable assistance to the authorities was the medical profession, mingling with the population and undoubtedly involved in the treatment of wounded men, but the deputy-lieutenant of the West Riding admitted their reluctance to give help, which was probably much more than a matter of professional ethics and personal interest.

The handling of the issue by sections of the press, the *Nottingham Review*, the *Leeds Mercury* and the *Manchester Commercial Advertiser*, indicates that a substantial and in-

fluential section of middle-class opinion was prepared to give
the Luddites a fair deal, to enquire into their grievances, to
look fairly objectively at what they were doing, and to refrain
from emotive, alarmist writing in the reporting of news. They
found the Luddites an object of pity as well as of blame, and
they lamented, in good Whig tradition, the opportunities that
were being provided for the domestic use of standing armies.
Even among those whose job it was to enforce the law against
the Luddites there was some disposition to treat them with
leniency; Luddism had its Nadin and Baron Wood, but it
had its Fitzwilliam, who managed to work for the suppression
of Luddites without ever hating them, and it had Judge Bailey,
whose supposed sympathy for them caused Joseph Radcliffe to
ask that he should be excluded from participation in the York
Assizes of January 1813. According to Radcliffe, the Luddites
called him their friend because of his leniency at the Nottinghamshire Lent Assizes of 1812. And it would not be difficult
to name individuals of social standing and political importance
who looked to the cause, rather than the crime, of Luddism.
Of these Lord Byron stands supreme for his memorable maiden
speech in the House of Lords.[14]

But given the weaknesses of the authorities, the forces at
their disposal, and a hostile public opinion, it must be acknowledged that Luddism was technically successful and difficult to prevent and eliminate because it happened where it
happened. Just as the geographical distribution of the industries concerned was in part responsible for the location of
Luddism, so was that location responsible for the intense
difficulty experienced in bringing it under control. It was
relatively simple to bring law and order to the town of Nottingham; there was a compact geographical area, a practised
magistracy, and a substantial middle class whose aid could be
enlisted as special constables or watch patrols. In consequence
there were relatively few breakings in Nottingham itself, though
the town was the main concentration point of the hosiery trade.
By contrast the country areas were virtually impossible to
police and control. The scattered villages might be many miles

from the nearest magistrate though within his jurisdiction, and responsibility devolved upon the village community, which would be solidly working-class and lacking a middle-class contingent to give some semblance of authority and command. In Yorkshire a similar situation existed. The big town, Leeds, remained relatively orderly and under control. Halifax, too, was not much of a problem in spite of the fears of some of its residents. It was in the straggling villages around Huddersfield, some of them miles from anywhere, that Luddism was most strongly established and most effective. And in Lancashire, though Manchester had its food riots, it was Westhoughton and Middleton that experienced Luddism. Nor is it surprising that the military authorities were reluctant to disperse small parties of soldiers amongst the hostile and unpoliced villages, isolating the law-bringers amidst an alien population.[15]

1   Baines, E. *History of the Cotton Manufacture in Great Britain* (1966 2nd edn) p 235; Thompson, E. P. *The Making . . . .* pp 554, 557; Darvall, F.O. *Popular Disturbances and Public Order . . . .* pp 66, 67, 68, 75; Bythell, D. *The Handloom Weavers* p 199
2   *Leeds Mercury,* 23 November 1811, 21 December 1811, 1 February 1812; Nottingham Borough Records, M429, F 24
3   *Manchester Mercury,* 5 May 1812
4   Darvall, F. O. *Popular Disturbances and Public Order . . . .* p 1; *Leeds Mercury,* 29 August 1812
5   *Leeds Mercury,* 22 February 1812; HO 42/123, Précis of troubles in Northern Counties, June 1812; Ibid, Hobhouse to HO, 30 May 1812; HO 42/132, Hobhouse to HO, 9 January 1813; Radcliffe MSS, 126/118; Peel, F. *The Risings of the Luddites* p 146
6   *Leeds Mercury,* 7 November 1812; Fitzwilliam MSS 45/134, 46/68; HO 42/123, Maitland to HO, 16 May 1812; HO 42/126, Maitland to HO, 5 August 1812; HO 42/123, Grey to HO, 8, 13 May 1812
7   HO 42/123, Maitland to HO, 4, 6 May 1812; ibid, Grey to HO, 8 May 1812; HO 42/138, Nadin to HO, 26 March 1814; HO 42/126, Lloyd to HO, 29, 31 August 1812; *Leeds Mercury,*

19 September 1812; HO 42/125, Maitland to HO, 18 July 1812; HO 42/130, Maitland to HO, 23 December 1812

8 HO 42/117, Wright to HO, 28 November 1811; Coldham to HO, December 1811; Middleton to HO, 12 December 1811; Smith to HO, 28 November 1811; Newcastle to HO, 2 December 1811; HO 42/120, Spencer to HO, 8 February 1812

9 HO 42/123, Maitland to HO, 4 May 1812; see account in Raynes, F. *Appeal to the Public* . . . .

10 *Leeds Mercury*, 28 December 1811; *Manchester Commercial Advertiser*, 28 April 1812; HO 40/1, Fletcher to HO, 26 April 1812; HO 42/120, Newcastle to HO, 14 February 1812; HO 40/1, Maitland to HO, 15 May 1812

11 HO 42/123, Hardy to HO, 19 May 1812; Fitzwilliam MSS 45/138, ibid 45/128; HO 42/122, Foster to HO, 20 April 1812; Fitzwilliam MSS 46/35; HO 42/121, Morgan to S. Perceval March 1812; HO 42/122, Clerk of the Peace Office, Wakefield, to HO, 29 April 1812; HO 42/123, Maitland to HO, 4, 6, 23 May 1812

12 HO 42/123, Maitland to HO, 4, 6 May 1812; eg Fitzwilliam MSS 46/34, 46/35; Radcliffe MSS 126/41; HO 42/122, Scatcherd to HO, 22 April 1812; Clerk of the Peace Office, Wakefield, to HO, 29 April; HO 42/123, Gordon to General Grey, 1 May 1812, Campbell to Grey, 1 May 1812

13 *Nottingham Journal*, 23 March 1811; *Leeds Mercury*, 29 February 1812; *Manchester Commercial Advertiser*, 3 March 1812

14 *Leeds Mercury*, 14 March 1812; Radcliffe MSS 126/102, Peel, F. *The Risings of the Luddites* p 67; HO 42/122, Ikin to Campbell, 15 April 1812; Fitzwilliam MSS 46/17; ibid, 46/88

15 HO 42/123, Maitland to HO, 4 May 1812

Chapter Six

LUDDISM AND THE MAKING OF THE ENGLISH WORKING CLASS

LUDDISM CAME TO an end, it has recently been suggested, not because of the success of the authorities in rounding up its leaders but because of a substantial improvement in the conditions which originally gave rise to Luddism. This is probably true. If the conditions had not changed, then other leaders would presumably have eventually emerged to carry on the struggle. On the other hand it seems beyond doubt that in Yorkshire, during the second half of 1812, and in Nottinghamshire during the second half of 1816, the authorities did succeed in tracking down and apprehending the main leaders, the removal of whom was believed to have dealt a killing blow to the organisation of machine-breaking in the respective areas. After Mellor and his associates had been hanged at York, it was reported from Huddersfield that the feelings of the people had, in consequence, subsided into a dead calm, all the croppers having the appearance of being ashamed of themselves; it is quite possible that the writer misinterpreted the appearance of the croppers. Earlier it was similarly believed that the executions at Lancaster and Chester had made a considerable impression on the people of those two disturbed counties. And later the removal of Jem Towle from the ranks of the Nottinghamshire Luddites, with his execution in November 1816, eliminated the remaining General Ludd or local leader, and the gang managed no more than a few desultory efforts after his loss. The execution of Towle, the Home Office was informed, had done great good and caused much alarm among the Luddites. In Yorkshire and Nottinghamshire, where organisation and leadership were important, the loss of vital leaders was an important factor in the timing of the ending of Luddism. In Lancashire and Cheshire, where Luddism arose largely from the unplanned behaviour of large crowds, a single magisterial coup against leaders would not make very much difference.

There seems little reason to suppose that the harsher legislation introduced by the government served either as a deterrent to would-be Luddites or as a means to the detection of established ones. On the other hand, the efficacy of the fast-moving military patrols which policed the troubled areas of Yorkshire and Lancashire in the summer and autumn of 1812 appears to have been both a deterrent to law-breakers and a means of breaking through local silence-barriers, helping in both the detection of past offenders and the discouragement of future ones. For all this, Luddism was essentially the product of economic distress, and it would be stopped only when economic conditions showed some improvement. As mentioned previously, Captain Macdougal, writing from Stalybridge, Cheshire, on 7 December 1812, reported that all was quiet in that part of the world and was likely to remain so as long as the cotton-masters were working long hours and the spinners were enjoying higher wages. From Yorkshire came similar reports that an improved state of trade had brought greater contentment and justified a happier prognosis for the state of public order in the winter ahead. The Whig critics who had condemned the Orders in Council were not unreasonably rejoicing that their repeal had gone a long way towards eliminating the popular discontent of which Luddism was a manifestation.[1]

It would be tempting to any admirer of the Luddites and their methods to see in the ending of Luddism a triumph for the tactics pursued by the militants. Collective bargaining by riot might have had its successes for Northumbrian miners in the eighteenth century, for Spitalfields silk workers, and even

West of England cloth workers, but it is difficult to see the apparent triumphs of the Luddites as anything more than the superficial appearance of victory. The men of Nottinghamshire, in Felkin's opinion, succeeded in the short term in obtaining a general two shillings (10p) per dozen rise in the price for manufacturing stockings, and they frightened some employers into a temporary abandoning of methods of cut-up production. Yet the rise was soon lost and the cut-ups were soon restored when the reign of terror came to an end.

Nor is there anything in the history of the next forty years to suggest that the Luddites achieved anything for the stockingers and lace workers. Wages continued to sink as the industry dropped deeper into depression, and the grievances of 1812 were still the grievances of 1845: cut-up production, truck-payments, improper abatements, employment of unskilled labour. If it is argued on the one hand that the state of the hosiery trade for the next forty years is poor testimony to the efficacy of laissez-faire principles, it must be conceded on the other that there was nothing in the Luddite programme that would have helped the revival of the industry. Abolition of cut-ups, which became the principle Luddite demand, would have severely damaged the industry at its one growing point and would have contributed nothing towards the raising of wages, which was the principle and ultimate aim behind all the demands of the Midlands Luddites. The terrorising of individual employers for a limited period of time did nothing to rouse hosiery from the torpor into which it had been gradually sinking for some years before Luddism, and in which it remained for many years after Luddism was at an end.[2]

In Lancashire the Luddites were ostensibly attempting to prevent the introduction of steam-loom weaving as a replacement for handloom weaving, and even for this grand, ambitious purpose there is some appearance of success. The 1792 attack on Grimshaw's factory in Manchester, which contained twenty-four Cartwright looms, did cause some fear that the attacks would be renewed when further experiments were undertaken, and both contemporaries and historians have seen this attack as the prime deterrent in inhibiting the extension of steam-loom weaving. Following the Middleton attack by the Luddites on 20 and 21 April 1812, it was reported that Daniel Burton & Son were not to work their looms any more, an evident triumph for Luddism, though the machine-breakers were paying a heavy price for victory according to the report elsewhere that four hundred people had been thrown out of work, reducing many families to great distress and causing many of Burton's workmen to flee the town with their families in the hope of finding work elsewhere. Still, this did give some substance to Luddite claims of victory and grounds for Halévy's view that the fear of machine-breaking was the main factor behind the manufacturers' reluctance to convert to power-loom weaving.

It is not, of course, possible to measure the extent of this fear or to estimate with any precision the consequence of it; what can be seen is that from the early 1820s, when the technical problems of manufacturing an efficient power-loom had been solved and normal peace conditions were offering settled trade prospects, there was apparently no hesitation in introducing power-looms in spite of the opposition that had previously been shown. This suggests that other factors than that of working-class opposition had previously operated to keep the power-loom out; foremost amongst these were the imperfections of the early machinery, which made it a dubious investment before 1820, and the plentiful supply of cheap labour, which, as in the hosiery trade, acted as a disincentive to technological change. And so for probably forty years after the invention of the power-loom by Cartwright in 1785 the growth of power-operators was paralleled by a growth of hand-operators, not because machine-breaking was a strong deterrent to the introduction of power-looms, but because the economic case for conversion to steam-loom weaving was sufficiently well-balanced to ensure a long lapse of time before power-weaving acquired parity and eventually superiority in numbers. Though handloom weavers continued to attack power-looms in years of distress, as in 1819 and 1826, machine-breaking was a negligible factor in explaining the delay in the transfer to power-weaving. The latter was in no sense a triumph for Luddism. It was, of course, argued earlier that it was not a real purpose of Luddism either, that there was no real prospect or intention of trying to prevent the use of steam looms. In this case, the success of the Luddites must again be sought in the wage levels which the handloom weavers achieved when their violent protests were over; and by this criterion they were as unsuccessful as the framework-knitters, experiencing an ever-declining status during the years in which they competed with power-operators before they were finally replaced and disappeared.[3]

Lancashire Luddism, as a shapeless protest movement, lacked the precise aims to permit the registering of measurable success. The West Riding was a more promising area for Luddite enterprise in that the croppers had for a long time fought a fairly successful rearguard action against the mechanisation of their part of the cloth-making industry. The cropper came nearest to the Luddite of popular imagination; he was neither the popular protest-maker nor the collective bargainer by riot, but rather the opponent of labour-saving machinery which threatened his very existence. When the croppers' opposition erupted into violence in 1812, a few victories were chalked up. On 25 March the Home Office was informed that Mr Taylor, a Horbury magistrate, had recommended the pulling down of obnoxious machinery in the area in order to placate the offended croppers. This unwelcome news constituted a tactical victory for Luddism, for most of the smaller operators, the owners of cropping-shops rather than the factory-owners who did their own finishing, were persuaded, either by actual visitations or the threat of them, to dismantle their shearing-frames. Lindsey of Gildersome, who held out longer than most, was not tackled until mid-September 1812; he got his machinery working again in spite of the threatening letters he continued to receive, though his courage was only as great as the military protection he was receiving, and he was contemplating stopping his own machinery once the troops were withdrawn. Even the bigger men could be successfully tackled. Thompsons of Rawdon and Fosters of Horbury received devastating visits from the Luddites; William Cartwright was driven to the verge of bankruptcy; and Horsfalls of Marsden were demoralised by the assassination of their head. On the death of William Horsfall, the use of obnoxious machinery was discontinued at Ottiwells mill, and hand-cropping was resumed; a few years later the Horsfalls disposed of their Marsden property. Such developments, together with the terror that the Leeds croppers continued to exercise over manufacturers in that town, suggest a fair measure of success for the Yorkshire Luddites, at least in their ability to strike at their enemies.

As an act of self-preservation, however, Yorkshire Luddism was no more than a short-term expedient which could not hope for more than short-term successes. It has been estimated that between 1806 and 1817 the number of gig-mills in Yorkshire increased from 5 to 72 and the number of shears operated by machinery from 100 to 1,462; of 3,378 surviving croppers 1,170 were totally and 1,445 partially employed. The craft disappeared, and croppers turned to any alternative form of employment they could find. It has been argued that at an earlier date the croppers were willing as a body to negotiate a phased introduction of machinery had the employers been prepared to meet them on this, but it is difficult to imagine their willingness to negotiate themselves totally out of existence, however gentle the phasing programme. The croppers disappeared, and no one would care to argue that gig-mills and shearing-frames were advantageous to them if only they had been able to take a longer or broader view; they might have been advantageous to the industry as a whole, but to the sectional interest of the croppers they were a disaster. Yet it does not take a doctrinaire advocate of laissez-faire economics to argue for redeployment of labour where techniques have become obsolete and men thereby redundant.[4]

If workmen did themselves no great good by breaking machines, it is also probably true that they did themselves

no great harm. Just as there were temporary triumphs regis-
tered over particular employers, so were there temporary
hardships to be borne as workshops closed down, but the
disastrous consequences forecast by some as the outcome of
Luddism do not appear to have been fulfilled. If technological
advance was slow in cotton-weaving, there were perfectly good
reasons why this was so, quite apart from any alarm which
innovators might have experienced at Luddite behaviour. And
if technological advances were impeded in Yorkshire, this was
a short-term affair and operated in a small geographical area,
the town of Leeds itself. It was the hosiery industry which
had the greatest fear that Luddism would deter investors,
cause a withdrawal of capital, and lead to the impoverish-
ment of the area. The *Leeds Mercury* at an early stage advanced the argument that Nottinghamshire Luddism would
drive manufacturers to areas where their capital might be employed safely and away from areas where it was at risk. A
classic example of this was when John Heathcoat of Loughborough moved his entire business down to Tiverton in Devon
after his lace factory had been attacked by Luddites in 1816.
In fact he had already decided to leave before the actual
attack took place. The loss to the area of Heathcoat, one of
the great innovators and the owner of the bobbin-net lace
patent, has in recent times been held up as a poor testimonial to
the efficacy of machine-breaking as a weapon of industrial
warfare. According to Felkin, Heathcoat's departure cost
Nottingham and district the employment and profit derived
from the working of 6-700 machines. One commentator
assessed this loss in terms of £10,000 a year in wages. Yet
this is only one side of the argument. Far from being driven
away from Nottingham and district by Luddism, the hosiery
and lace trades became increasingly concentrated in the Midlands to the detriment of other provincial centres which had
not experienced Luddism, and Heathcoat, by cutting himself
off from the main stream of developments in the lace trade,
probably put an effective end to his own career as an inventor.
He certainly did not put an end to trade developments in

Loughborough, where another firm moved into his vacated premises and the lace trade continued to give employment to increasing numbers of the town's population.

Nor was it the fault of the Luddites that the hosiery trade failed to make the technological advance that other textile trades experienced in the century 1750-1850. The traditional domestic structure of the industry, the over-abundant labour supply sustaining it, and the evil of frame-rents, which gave manufacturers a vested interest in the status quo, all retarded the arrival of a factory-based industry operating power-driven machinery. The Midlands Luddites were not part of an 'anti-machine' movement, but their employers were during the following forty years, to the great cost of the workmen.[5]

Many of the homilies directed against the working classes, via the Luddites, were, in fact, either misplaced or misleading or both. According to the *Manchester Commercial Advertiser,* any invention for the abridging of human labour was 'infallibly followed by an increase of wages to artisans of every description'. This might have been what some people cared to believe, or at least wanted others to believe, but it was demonstrably not so. It was no more than a propaganda statement, giving a gloss and a corruption to an argument that might very reasonably have been made, namely that labour-saving machines, though creating hardship to some in the short-term, were generally good for the industry concerned and conducive to eventual all-round prosperity, even for those whose skill was being supplanted. A similarly cosy message was transmitted by the *Leeds Mercury* on the same theme; the labouring classes were deceiving themselves, it suggested, since the interests of the rich and the poor were not in opposition to each other. If there were no rich the poor would be still poorer. A philosophic basis for the optimist school of thinkers on the Industrial Revolution was already being laid; but whatever the relationship between riches and poverty in general it could hardly be demonstrated in the short run that the interests of the innovators were the same as those of the people whom the innovations were displacing. It is not reasonable to say

that the Luddites of 1812 should have been prepared to ignore
their own short-term comforts for the benefit of later generations and that they chose instead to prejudice the chances of
future working men by adopting a short-sighted attitude; they
operated within their own immediate context and not within
the context of long-term industrial development. They were
tactically wrong in believing that they could successfully resist
mechanisation in their own industries, but they were not
morally wrong to wish to do this when their very existence
might seem to be, and might in fact be, threatened. Luddism
was not a justifiable exercise in that its results justified it, but it
was justifiable in that it seemed worthwhile to those who opted
for it.[6]

It is tempting, but wrong, to find validity in Luddite arguments and justification for Luddite conduct in the later history
of industries which failed to respond to Luddite pressures and
whose workmen suffered subsequent decline in their fortunes.
There is no necessary causal connection between the failure of
Luddism and this decline. It is incontestable that framework-
knitters suffered degradation during the next thirty years without the presence of powered machinery in their industry, but
this observation is irrelevant and mistakes the nature of the
dilemma. Powered machinery, housed in factories, was to be
the salvation of the industry in the 1850s and might have been
so a generation earlier had it been introduced. The Luddites,
by contrast, had no proposals that would have contributed to
rousing hosiery from its state of torpor and had some, the
prohibition of cut-ups for instance, that might have killed it off
completely. Again, the decline and disappearance of the handloom weavers and croppers are not in question; the croppers
were right to think that mechanisation was causing their pre-
dicament, though the weavers were almost certainly wrong
in 1812, but it could hardly be argued from this that power-
looms should not have been introduced or that woollen cloth
should have gone on being cropped by hand-shears. The Luddites were not necessarily right because those who opposed
them failed to prevent industrial stagnation or to solve the

social problems involved in redundancy over the next decades.[7]

If the Luddites of 1812 were slow to learn their economic lessons about the impossibility of resistance to technological change, workmen of later generations have been equally slow. The debate about machines replacing men has continued, and the age of automation poses threats of redundancy to individual workmen as did the earlier ages of industrial invention. The debate is now, of course, conducted within an entirely different moral and political climate. Changing attitudes and the strength of working-class organisation ensure that men who yield to machines usually do so without violence and in consequence of negotiated agreements by means of which financial compensation goes to the displaced. The implementation of technological change involves much more study than simply consideration of the economic factors involved. There is, too, the further consideration that efficiency and profit have to be measured in social rather than individual terms; a machine which cuts down human labour for the sole purpose of increasing profits lacks the moral justification of a machine which, for instance, reduces the labour-hours of the population. The questions of who benefits from labour-saving devices and who might conceivably lose are ones that must now be considered in detail; it is no longer enough to believe and to preach that what is good for the manufacturer must necessarily be good for the rest of the population. Society as a whole demands to feel the benefits from, even to exercise control over, the workings of labour-saving machinery.

But the change has been a slow one, and machine-breaking did not come to an end when Jem Towle and others responsible for the attack on Heathcoat's mill at Loughborough in June 1816 were eventually hanged for their offence. Occasional attacks continued to be made on stocking and lace frames after this time, since it presumably still seemed a convenient way of making an employer pay for a particular sin, though the atttacks were too spasmodic to invalidate the view that Luddism came to an end in 1816. And there were still occasions, in other industries, where machine-breaking, like collective-bargaining by riot, formed a useful supplement to more constitutional methods of trade-union pressure after the Combination Acts had been repealed in 1824, for legality or near-legality were themselves no guarantee of effectiveness. In 1831, for instance, coal-miners on strike at Bedlington wrecked the pit winding gear as a particularly effective way of ensuring that the mine did not work while they themselves remained on strike. Two years earlier, in 1829, there had been attacks on certain Manchester weaving-sheds, employing not power-looms but handlooms, the owners of which had recently reduced piece-rates. This was a classic example, in the best Nottingham-shire Luddite tradition, of striking at the underpaying master. And the practice of interfering with machinery as a means of ensuring trade-union solidarity during industrial disputes also extended well into the nineteenth century in the shape of 'rattening' in parts of the Sheffield cutlery trade in the 1860s, which involved interference with the tools used by workmen who refused to fall into line.[8]

Collective bargaining by riot would eventually be replaced by other forms of collective bargaining, and negotiated, phased acceptance of new machinery would eventually replace machine-breaking, but hostility to new machinery which found its expression in wrecking also survived Luddism by a number of years. This has recently been labelled a 'less sophisticated' object for the machine-breakers than the pressure they attempted to put on employers on other occasions. The two outstanding examples of anti-machinery riots occurred in 1826 and 1830. If the advent of the power-loom could be said to be largely irrelevant to the problems of the cotton weavers in 1812, the same could not be said about their troubles in 1826. The years 1821-5 witnessed the first large-scale adoption of the power-loom, which intensified competition among both employers and workers for the work available. The years of competition from the power-loom and the sharp fall in the price of cotton culminated in 1826 in the worst depression known to the industry, and not surprisingly the handloom weavers saw a strong causal connection between the develop-

L

ments they were witnessing and experiencing. The fate of the handloom weavers has been described as the largest case of technological unemployment in recent economic history, and in three days in April 1826 they made their vain bid to stave off this fate when the country weavers of the small north Lancashire cotton towns, Blackburn, Darwen, Bacup, Bury, Rawtenstall, and Harlingham, broke power-looms in their distress and anger.

This 'massive display of resentment on the part of the entire community' did not of course, destroy the power-loom or limit its extended use, and, though there were further fears of public disorder in 1829, the violence of 1826 was not repeated. Machine-breaking had not apparently achieved anything, it did not stop further investment in power-loom factories, and it had revealed the impossibility of the complete, simultaneous destruction of obnoxious machinery needed to make such a campaign effective. Other attempts at resisting machinery were made, such as the attack of ribbon-weavers on Beck's Coventry factory in 1831, but machine-breaking as an attempt to resist the mechanisation of industrial processes was essentially at an end. Developments in mechanisation still, of course, induced fears that were far from being irrational. In 1834, for instance, woollen weavers in Bradford complained that improvements in mechanisation seemed to have as their object the adaptation of machinery to the youngest class of workers, thereby threatening the status of the adult workman. But the last extensive and the most successful machine-breaking outburst of them all, the labourers' risings of 1830, which dealt the threshing-machine a blow from which it never recovered, was not an industrial riot but one of farm labourers. Ludd's real name might have been Captain Swing, but this only confirms the relevance of Luddism to those societies where the patterns of industrialisation were incomplete.[9]

The Luddites are not to be scorned because they did not follow the more sophisticated techniques and practices of their successors, who organised trade unions or entered politics to secure legal guarantees of labour rights. On the other hand it would be unduly romantic to suppose that industrial sabotage had a useful part to play in future attempts by the working classes to agitate for their various causes. It is not necessary to be either Whiggish or Fabian to reject industrial sabotage and violence as a 'primitive' form of behaviour and a way of solving labour problems inferior to the methods employed by men who later built up powerful trade unions or attempted to use the power of the state on behalf of their sectional interests. Just as war is an irrational and immoral way of trying to solve international disagreement, so is a reversion to the techniques and methods of the uncivilised barbarian, controlled and limited by the Luddites as they are controlled and limited by the makers of warfare, a less rational and less morally acceptable way of trying to solve industrial disputes than that which relies on voting power or, in a situation of intolerability, the power to withdraw labour.

Nor can the Luddites be held contemptible because part of their efforts was concerned with resisting technological change. It was morally no more reprehensible to wish to preserve the status of a dying craft than to wish to increase profits through mechanical innovations, and the techniques employed by both parties to achieve their aims were not deserving respectively of moral censure and moral approbation. The romantic might wish to argue that pre-industrial society was preferable to that which followed the Industrial Revolution, that society's losses have outweighed the material gains which industrialisation has brought, yet this argument, whatever its interest, is of no relevance to an assessment of Luddite achievements. Luddism did not pose a stark choice between two absolute, diametrically-opposed alternatives of industrial change, with all it involved, on the one hand, and man in a state of nature on the other. It was conducted inside the context of the Industrial Revolution and was not a desire to opt out. Perhaps it is to rationalise Luddite motivation too much and to make too much clear sense out of a welter of confusion to suggest that Luddism represented an alternative morality to laissez-faire, for there was no antithesis of altruism and selfishness between the two; but Luddism did at least indicate that there was a working-class voice which demanded to be heard, or an 'alternative political economy' to be considered. It was unfortunate for Luddite prospects of success that this was only the voice of the residual crafts and not that of groups more central and vital to the carrying-forward of the Industrial Revolution.

Luddism was, in places, a remarkably successful exercise of working-class solidarity and excellent testimony to what could be carried out by organisation. When its lessons had been learned, adapted, and adopted by groups more vitally important to the economy than disappearing croppers, redundant handloom weavers, or cottage stocking-knitters, it might then be said to have contributed something to the making of the English working class. In the context of 1811-16 its contribution can be assessed only in terms of the vague concept of working-class 'culture'. Luddism was, it has been argued, 'a manifestation of working-class culture of greater independence and complexity' than any known in the previous century, though this possibly arises from the fact that the 'years of illegal tradition before 1811 are years of a richness at which we can only guess'. In making their contribution to this 'manifestation of working-class culture', George Mellor, the assassin of William Horsfall, and James Towle, the leader of the Loughborough attack of June 1816, become 'men of heroic stature'. Over this the historian is in a quandary. On the one hand he is anxious to accept all the help he can get from the sociologist in refining his concepts; on the other he usually wants to say what he means and to communicate his thought in intelligible language. If working-class culture comprises all that the working class thought and did, then Luddism adds a new dimension to it. If years of 'illegal tradition' are thought to have a particular 'richness', then the years of Luddism were bumper years in which working-class culture flourished in an unprecedented manner.

Yet there must remain some doubt of the value to the historian of this concept of working-class culture. It is difficult to see, for instance, that much progress has in fact been made beyond being able to argue that some working-class people acted illegally during this period and that by so doing they posed a more serious challenge to society than had previously been posed from working-class ranks. It can hardly be argued that some new pattern of working-class behaviour was established which determined the nature of working-class participation in industrial or political affairs in the future.[10]

If the economic consequences of Luddism were slight, there is some reason to suppose that its political consequences were of some importance at least in the short run. These are not to be judged in terms of the supposed revolutionary movement of which the Luddites were thought, by some, to be a part, but in terms of the impact made upon political society by the Luddites' successful challenge to the forces of authority. The liberal press might regret the occurrence of Luddism because an excuse had been given for the use of military force against a popular cause, which could only end in victory for the authorities and damage to all popular causes such as that of parliamentary reform, which was beginning to re-emerge in the latter stages of the wars; yet the reforming liberal was glad enough to see the military forces of the country restore peace and tranquillity and remove the threat to property rights. As William Dawson of Wakefield wrote to Fitzwilliam on 3 May, the gentlemen of respectability who had been steady opponents of the government up to that point now saw the need to present a united front against this apparent threat to society. The mill-owner might have campaigned against the Orders in Council and supported peace movements in opposition to loyalist gentry and parsons, but William Cartwright of Rawfolds Mill was happy enough to have the assistance of the Rev Hammond Roberson of near-by Healds Hall, the bellicose Tory parson of Liversedge, who was the principal local worthy to take a lead against the Luddites in the Spen Valley. Differences could be buried while such a foe was knocking at the gate.

The alliance was mutually advantageous. For the government supporters it was good to witness the 'ultimate loyalty of manufacturers when faced with working-class Jacobinism'. The manufacturers for their part made sizeable gains; at the local level the paternalistic squire who might have sympathised with the hungry worker was alienated by his riotous behaviour and became more sympathetic to the position of the industrialist; at the national level the ministry 'found it convenient to accept arguments of "free competition" out of sheer counter-revolutionary opportunism'. With this new alliance forming around them, the Luddites found themselves 'opposed on one side by the values of order, on the other by the values of economic freedom'.[11]

The clearest case of realignment prompted by Luddism is to be seen in Nottingham, where a Whig corporation had voiced strong opposition to entry into war in 1793 and had been labelled 'Jacobin' in consequence, and where opposition to the government had been a steady feature of corporation politics throughout the previous twenty years, except when the threat of French invasion hung over the country in 1804-5. According to local Tories the reforming chickens were now coming home to roost; the 'jacobinical principles with which the inferior orders have been sedulously inoculated' were now being turned against those who had previously enunciated them. Town clerk George Coldham saw the political menace of Luddism clearly enough; if Luddism were to be successful in its limited industrial ends, he wrote, the workmen would go further and there was no saying what might be the next object of their vengeance. The use of force as a means of achieving one's aims was no part of Coldham's creed. A wedge was being driven between the working classes of Nottingham and their Whig leaders, as the latter were being driven to demand vigorous action and intervention from the Home Office authorities, their traditional enemies. The fright which they had received from the Luddites caused the Whigs to suspect the anti-war protests of May 1815 as the work of radicals and revolutionaries, and made them very susceptible to revolution gossip throughout the immediate post-war period, collaborating with the central government in staging, rather than preventing, the pathetic Pentrich rebellion of June 1817. Whatever the justification of 'Jacobin' taunts twenty years previously, Luddism ensured that the reforming ambitions of Nottingham's leaders would in the future be worked out along thoroughly peaceful and constitutional lines, and it would be no exaggeration to find the political consequences of Luddism still expressing themselves as late as the Chartist period, when Feargus O'Connor got himself elected as one of Nottingham's MPs on a mixture of working-class and Tory support. But the abortive industrial campaigns of 1811-16 were to be followed by the abortive political ones of 1831-2 before the working classes were again to strike out in relative independence on the enterprise of Chartism.[12]

1   Webb, R. K. *Modern England, from the 18th Century to the Present* (1969) p 147; HO 40/2, Allison to HO, 16 January 1813; Report of House of Lords Committee of Secrecy, July 1812; HO 40/3(1), Extracts of letter received from Nottingham, 2 December 1816; HO 40/2, Macdougal to HO, 7 December 1812, eg HO 40/2, Chesterton at Leeds to HO, 9 January 1813
2   Felkin, W. *History of the Machine Wrought Hosiery* .... p 439; Thompson, E. P. *The Making* .... p 551
3   Bythell, D. *The Handloom Weavers* pp 6, 74; *Leeds Mercury,* 25 April 1812; *Manchester Mercury,* 28 April 1812
4   HO 42/121, Campbell to HO, 25 March 1812; HO 40/2, Raynes to HO throughout September 1812; Sykes, D. F. E. *The History of Huddersfield and its Vicinity* (1898) p 285; Thompson, E. P. *The Making* .... pp 550-551; ibid p 526
5   *Leeds Mercury,* 18 December 1811; Felkin, W. *History of the Machine Wrought Hosiery* .... p 242; *Nottingham Journal,* 9 November 1816; Chambers, J. D. *The Vale of Trent 1670-1800* (1957) p 60; Hammond, J. L. and B. *The Skilled Labourer* p 243; *Nottingham Review,* 26 July 1816, 8 May 1818
6   *Manchester Commercial Advertiser,* 21 April 1812; *Leeds Mercury,* 2 May 1812
7   Thompson, E. P. *The Making* .... p 551
8   Hobsbawm, E. J. *The Machine Breakers*; Bythell, D. *The*

Handloom Weavers p 204; Thompson, E. P. *The Making* . . . .
p 552

9 Bythell, D. *The Handloom Weavers* pp 72, 139, 197-203;
   Prest, J. *Industrial Revolution in Coventry* (1960) p 48; Hobsbawm, E. J. *The Machine Breakers*

10 Thompson, E. P. *The Making* . . . . pp 543, 552, 592, 601

11 Fitzwilliam MSS 45/135, W. Dawson to Fitzwilliam, 3 May
    1812; Thompson, E. P. *The Making* . . . . pp 545, 546, 561

12 Newcastle MSS NeC 4919b, J. T. Becher to Newcastle, 12
    February 1812; HO 42/117, Coldham to HO, December 1811

APPENDIX

Diary of Events, 1811-17

1811

11 March. Protest meeting in Nottingham market-place and breaking of about sixty frames at Arnold.

16-23 March. Outrages in many villages in the north-west. More than 100 frames broken, including Sutton-in-Ashfield, Kirby, Woodborough, Lambley, Bulwell, and Ilkeston in Derbyshire.

29 March. Frame-breaking at Mansfield.

13 April. Reward of 100 guineas offered after destruction of six frames at Bulwell.

14 July. Destruction of frames at Sutton-in-Ashfield (Kirby-in-Ashfield according to one account).

4 November. Six frames broken at Bulwell.

10 November. Attack on house of person named Hollingworth at Bulwell, involving death of a Luddite, John Westley of Arnold, who was shot as he entered the house. Ten to twelve frames broken at Kimberley, allegedly for the employment of colts.

12 November. Eight or nine frames broken at Basford.

13 November. Some fifty-four to seventy frames broken at Sutton-in-Ashfield.

18 November. One wide frame broken at Old Radford. Many threatening letters received. Rick-burning at Mansfield, Snein-

ton, and Hucknall Torkard; victims supposed to be those active against the frame-breakers.

23 November. One frame broken in Nottingham, one at Ilkeston.

23/24 November. Thirty to thirty-four frames broken at Basford in various workshops. One broken at Chilwell during the same night.

25 November. Eleven frames broken at Basford during the afternoon, several broken in Nottingham itself. Reports of breakings at Eastwood, Heanor and Cossall.

27 November. Frame broken at Carlton. Day-time attack on frames being transported under escort at Redhill.

28 November. Four frames broken at Basford, and three to five at Bobbers Mill.

29 November. Sixteen to eighteen frames broken at Beeston, nine to twelve at Blidworth, one at New Basford.

30 November. One frame broken at New Basford, two at Bobbers Mill, one at Old Radford, one at New Radford.

1 December. Two frames broken in Nottingham, eight at New Radford.

2 December. Two frames broken in Nottingham, two at Sneinton, five at New Radford.

3 December. One frame broken in Nottingham, twenty at Shepshead in Leicester. Threatening letters in Leicester, but in general stockingers peaceable and orderly. Around thirty frames broken at Ilkeston, one at South Wingfield, one at Wessington.

5 December. One frame broken in Nottingham, several at Basford.

6 December. Seven frames broken at Holbrook, eighteen at Pentrich.

7 December. Six frames broken at Bulwell, four at Arnold, ten at Pentrich.

11 December. Several frames broken at Ripley, one at Burton Joyce.

12 December. Stacks fired at Basford and one frame destroyed at Benton. Attacks also reported in Hucknall Torkard, Ilkes-

ton, Makeney, Heage, Holbrook, Crich, Swanwick, Riddings in Derbyshire.

14 December. Three frames broken in Nottingham.

15 December. Several frames broken in Nottingham, including lace-frames.

16 December. Rick-burning at Basford.

21-28 December. Robberies in Derbyshire by 'Ned Ludd's men' and frame-breakings in Nottingham, Basford and Arnold.

1812

1-4 January. Property attacks on the Notts/Derbyshire border.

2 January. One frame broken at Wollaton.

3 January. Nine frames broken at Basford, two at Bulwell.

4 January. Seven frames broken at Hucknall Torkard, two lace-frames in Nottingham.

5 January. Two lace-frames broken in Nottingham, belonging to person allegedly guilty of truck-payments, two at Old Radford.

6 January. Thirteen frames broken at Old Radford, five at Arnold.

4-11 January. Outrages included attack on the windmill on Bulwell Forest and frame-breaking at Heanor, Derbyshire.

11 January. One lace-frame broken at New Radford.

12 January. Eight lace-frames, making single press lace, broken at Nottingham.

13 January. Four warp-lace frames of truck-paying employer broken at New Radford.

14 January. Two frames broken at Sneinton. Holders accused of working at abated prices.

18 January. One frame broken at Nottingham.

19 January. Four frames broken at New Radford, including what was alleged to be the most complete silk frame in existence, two or three at Ruddington, nine warp-lace frames at Linby, seven cotton frames at Ilkeston, eleven at Swanwick.

20 January. Breaking at Arnold.

23 January. Twenty-two frames broken at Lenton, a quarter-

mile from the barracks. Carrier attacked outside Nottingham and frames en route from Kimberley destroyed.

24 January. Two frames broken at Radford.

25 January. Carrier from Sutton-in-Ashfield was stopped and had his cut-up hosiery goods destroyed, the rest being left untouched. Twenty-six frames broken at Clifton, fourteen at Ruddington.

26 January. Up to forty-five frames broken at Bagthorp and Underwood, three at Basford, one at Bulwell.

27 January. Three frames broken at Basford.

29 January. One frame broken at New Basford.

1-7 February. Breakings reported at Bobbers Mill, Basford, Heanor, and Burton Joyce, but a quieter week on the whole than the previous one.

10 February. One frame broken at Hucknall Torkard.

11 February. Opening of Gravener Henson's campaign to secure Parliamentary regulation of hosiery and lace trades.

14 February. Two frames broken at Hucknall Torkard. Proposed legislation announced by Government to make frame-breaking a capital offence.

17 February. One frame broken at Stanton, Derbyshire.

21 February. Five warp-frames broken in Nottingham.

7 March. Ten frames broken at Pentrich, two at Losco.

17 March. County Assizes. Benjamin Hancock, 21, and Joseph Peck, 17, sentenced to 14 years transportation; Gervas Marshall, 17, George Green, 21, and Robert Poley, 16, sentenced to 7 years transportation. A few others were acquitted.

27 April. Attempted assassination by shooting of a Nottingham hosier, William Trentham, who denied the allegation that he had 'abated' his men.

14 May. Loughborough Market riot.

25 July. Henson's Bill, mutilated by the House of Commons, is rejected by the House of Lords.

11 September. Bread riot in Nottingham.

3 November. Potato riot in Nottingham.

22 November. Lace-frame broken in Nottingham, which 'Ned Ludd had learnt was at work for half goods and half money'.

6 December. Abortive attack on frames in New Sneinton.

13 December. Cotton lace-frame, allegedly working under price, destroyed in New Radford.

19 December. Cotton lace-frame broken in Nottingham.

21 December. Lace-frame broken at Beeston for working under price.

1813

1 January. Ten frames reported broken at Melbourne, Derbyshire, in previous week.

3 January. Three silk-frames broken in Nottingham.

10 January. A wide cotton-frame destroyed in Nottingham.

13 November. Frames broken at Wimeswold, because of alleged employment of 'colts'.

1814

7 April. Seven frames broken at Kimberley over failure to secure an advance.

10 April. Twelve warp lace-frames broken at Castle Donington, allegedly at the Union Society's instigation.

11 April. Five silk-frames broken in Nottingham.

12 April. Abortive attack in Nottingham.

8 May. Four silk-frames broken in Nottingham.

26 July. Four lace-frames broken in Old Sneinton and one in New Sneinton. Also a few frames broken in Nottingham.

4 September. Fifteen stocking-frames broken in Old and New Basford, mainly two-needle cotton-frames.

14 October. Murder of William Kilby and abortive attempt on life of Thomas Garton of New Basford. Samuel Bamford, one of the attackers, was also slain. The incident was believed to have arisen as a result of information having been passed to the authorities concerning the illegal activities of James Towle.

1815

March. Lent Assizes. James Towle found 'not guilty' of frame-breaking. Judge indicates disagreement with verdict by warning Towle against the continuance of such practices.

24 April. George Coldham, town clerk of Nottingham, reports to Home Secretary 'Our old enemies the Luddites are at it again', but reference is only to a meeting held on the forest.

1816

11 May. One lace-frame broken at Loughborough.

13 May. Further breaking at Loughborough.

8-9 June. Twelve point-net lace-frames broken at New Radford and some yards of material stolen.

28 June. Attack on Heathcoat and Boden's mill at Loughborough, the greatest of the Luddite coups in the Midlands and the only one to compare with the factory assaults in Yorkshire and Lancashire. There were said to be seventeen in the gang of attackers, many from Nottingham, seven of whom, including James Towle, were later executed. The raid was probably the result of wage disputes, but there were allegations that trade rivalries occasioned this attack upon the owner of the patent for bobbin-net lace. Damage done was in the region of £6-8,000, and Heathcoat subsequently left the area, removing to Tiverton, which borough he was to represent in Parliament alongside Palmerston.

10 July. Shepshead, Leicestershire. Removal of jack-wires from eighteen frames.

3 October. Two frames broken in Nottingham.

14 October. Report of breaking of thirty frames at Lambley. Threatening letters still being received by hosiers.

2 November. Report of breaking of four wide frames at Bulwell.

14 November. Seven frames damaged in Leicester, supposedly by a youth who worked at the establishment concerned. No connection with Luddism believed to exist.

YORKSHIRE

1812

15 January. Leeds meeting of clothworkers, some with blackened faces and stated to be armed with hammers and clubs. James Shaw apprehended and committed. Information given on oath to Leeds magistrates of conspiracy to destroy machinery in certain mills. No attacks made following meeting.

19 January. Leeds. Oatlands Mill, near Woodhouse Carr, the property of Messrs Oates, Wood & Smithson, was discovered on fire. Contained gig-mills. Believed to be act of incendiarism as no one had worked there that day, Sunday, and combustible materials were discovered in several places.

22 February. Huddersfield. Attack on dressing-shop of Joseph Hirst of Marsh; shearing-frames destroyed. Similar attack on workshop of James Balderson of Crosland Moor. Luddites organised in two parties, the attackers and the watchmen.

26 February. Huddersfield. Attack on dressing-shop of William Hinchliffe of Leymoor. All machinery destroyed. Committee of manufacturers and merchants formed in Huddersfield with large discretionary powers.

5 March. Huddersfield. Four houses entered near Slaithwaite and frames and shears destroyed.

11 March. Huddersfield. Houses of John Garner of Honley, Clement Dyson of Dungeon, and Mr Roberts of Crosland, attacked and obnoxious machinery destroyed.

15 March. Huddersfield. Workshop of Francis Vickerman of Taylor Hill attacked, twenty to thirty pairs of shears broken, woollen cloth destroyed, and private property in house destroyed.

23/4 March. Rawdon. Attack on shearing-mill of William Thompson & Bros. Thirty to forty pairs of shears destroyed in twenty-minute attack. Thirty-six windows broken and three pieces of fine woollen cloth damaged.

25 March. Leeds. Dickenson, Carr & Co's workshop attacked and eighteen pieces of dressed cloth destroyed.

1 April. Special General Sessions of the Peace to institute Watch and Ward.

5 April. Huddersfield. Mr Smith of Snowgatehead, near Holmfirth, had all his dressing-frames and shears broken. Joseph Brook of Horn Coat suffered attacks on his frames, shears, household furniture and windows. James Brook of Honley had the shearing-frame he had owned for five weeks destroyed.

9 April. Wakefield. Attack on the Horbury Mill of Joseph Foster. Crowd, variously estimated at 3-600, said to possess firearms, hatchets and clubs, destroyed gig-mills, cropping shears and frames, and cloth, but ignored scribbling-machines. Guns were fired but with no apparent attempt to injure; windows broken. Crowd seen to disperse in various directions towards Wakefield, Leeds, Halifax, and Huddersfield. Estimated cost of damage £700.

11 April. Spen Valley. Attack on Rawfolds Mill of William Cartwright by a crowd of around 150 men gathered from various parts of woollen district. Mill was stoutly, if not strongly, defended. Luddites met first serious armed resistance and suffered first defeat. Some damage was done to the exterior of the mill, but no machinery was broken. Two of the assailants were killed and others wounded. With this abortive attack, Yorkshire machine-breaking was virtually at an end and Luddism acquired new patterns.

14 April. Sheffield and Rotherham food riots.

15 April. Barnsley food riot.

18 April. Attempted assassination of William Cartwright en route from Huddersfield.

27 April. Huddersfield. Assassination of William Horsfall, owner of shearing-frames and active pursuer of Luddites.

May. Arms raids, robberies, and reports of drillings, throughout the cloth areas. Eleven pairs of Cartwright's shears taken from grinders in Wakefield and smashed.

June. Continuation of arms raids but with greater emphasis on common robbery.

July. Still some robberies, but substantial order being restored.
13 August. Knottingley. Women almost organised a bread-riot.
18 August. Leeds. Corn Market riot of women and boys led by Lady Ludd. Meal shops threatened.
Sheffield. Food riots, directed against flour and meal sellers.
3 September. Halifax. Destruction of gig-mill at Southowram.
Gildersome. Destruction of shearing-frames at the workshop of Mr Lindsey.

1813

January. York Assizes. Three men convicted and executed for the murder of William Horsfall, five for the Rawfolds job, and nine more for stealing arms or money.
March. Bulk of forces withdrawn.

LANCASHIRE AND CHESHIRE

1811

December. Stockport. Rumours of presence of Nottingham delegates.

1812

January. More rumours.
February. Threatening letters sent to Stockport manufacturers employing steam-looms. Peter Marsland of Stockport reports attempt to fire his factory. Subscriptions alleged to be solicited in Manchester and Stockport on behalf of Nottingham Luddites.
20 March. Stockport. Large-scale attack on factory of William Radcliffe, inventor of dressing-machine which improved Cartwright's power-loom. Building saved from attempted destruction by fire.
6 April. R. A. Fletcher, magistrate of Bolton, informs Home Office of plans to fire Westhoughton mills.
8 April. Manchester. Exchange riots. Partly political in origin.

M

In later stages involved attack on factory of Mr Schofield, Newton Street, said to contain obnoxious machinery. Windows broken, but arrival of soldiers prevented destruction of factory.

9 April. Intended date for the destruction of Westhoughton mills.

14 April. Stockport riots. Attack on house and steam looms of J. Goodair. Houses of other steam-loom owners, Marsland, Hindley and Radcliffe, also attacked.

15 April. Macclesfield riots.

18 April. Manchester food riots.

19 April. Dean Moor meeting. Second abortive attempt to organise destruction of Westhoughton mills.

20 April. Food riots in Manchester, Oldham, Bolton, Ashton, and north-east Cheshire villages. Attack on Burton's Mill at Middleton, in part a sequel to the Oldham food riots. Colliers from Hollinwood and other rioters from Saddleworth marched from Oldham to Middleton and joined local crowds to attack Burton's power-loom factory. Five attackers were killed, many injured, and crowd withdrew.

21 April. Resumption of attack at Middleton. Some 200 men returned and burned down Burton's house. Military opened fire and there were perhaps six more deaths amongst the assailants. Tintwistle food riots.

24 April. Final and successful attack on Westhoughton. The origins and organisation of the successful attackers and their possible connections with the earlier abortive attempts are not clear.

1 May. The threatened day of the general rising.

25 May. Opening of Cheshire Assizes. Three men capitally convicted for attacks on machinery but respited.

May/June. Lancashire Assizes. Convictions not obtained against the six charged with arson at Middleton. Four were convicted and hanged for Westhoughton.

June. Raids for arms, robberies, and rumours of drilling.

27 August. Trial and acquittal of the Manchester '38' at Lancaster. Troop movements but few acts of disorder by this stage.

BIBLIOGRAPHY

PRIMARY SOURCES
MANUSCRIPT
   Home Office Papers
HO 40. Correspondence and papers, Disturbances
HO 42. Correspondence and Papers, Domestic and General
         George III Correspondence, 1782-1820
Treasury Solicitors' Papers (TS)
Fitzwilliam MSS
Newcastle MSS (NeC)
Radcliffe MSS
Nottingham Borough Records. Framework-knitters' Papers,
                            1812-14
                            Letters from London Police
                            Officers, M429
Place Collection. Additional MSS 27798-27817

PRINTED
   Official
Parliamentary Debates
Parliamentary Papers

   Newspapers
Leeds Intelligencer
Leeds Mercury
Manchester Commercial Advertiser

Manchester Mercury
Nottingham Journal
Nottingham Review

Other near-contemporary writing

Baines, E. *History of the Cotton Manufacture in Great Britain* (1835)

Blackner, J. *History of Nottingham* (1815)

Felkin, W. *History of the Machine-wrought Hosiery and Lace Manufacturers* (1867, reprinted Newton Abbot 1967)

Historical Account of the Luddites of 1811, 1822, and 1813 with Report of their Trials (Huddersfield 1862)

Knight, J. (intro) *The Trial at Full Length of the 38 Men from Manchester*

Parsons, E. *History of Leeds* (1834)

Raynes, F. *An Appeal to the Public, containing an account of Services rendered during the Disturbances in the North of England in the year 1812* (1817)

Sutton, J. F. *The Date Book of Nottingham, 1750-1850* (1852)

Secondary Works of particular help

Bythell, D. *The Handloom Weavers* (1969)

Chambers, J. D. 'The Vale of Trent, 1670-1800', *Economic History Review* Supplement 3, (1957)

Crump, W. B. *The Leeds Woollen Industry* (1931)

Crump, W. B. and Gorbal, G. *History of the Huddersfield Woollen Industry* (1935)

Darvall, F. O. *Popular Disturbances and Public Order in Regency England* (1934)

Hammond, J. L. & B. *The Skilled Labourer, 1760-1832* (1919)

Hobsbawm, E. J. *The Machine Breakers, Past & Present* (1952) 1

Peel, F. *The Risings of the Luddites* (1880)

Peel, F. *Spen Valley Past and Present* (1893)

Rudé, G. F. E. *The Crowd in History*. (1964)

Russell, J. 'The Luddites', *Transactions of the Thoroton Society* (1906)

Thompson, E. P. *The Making of the English Working Class* (1963)
Wadsworth, A. P. and Mann, J. D. L. *The Cotton Trade and Industrial Lancashire, 1660-1780* (1931)

ACKNOWLEDGEMENTS

I should like to thank Miss Betty Neech, and the staff of the Public Record Office, Nottingham City and University Libraries, Leeds City and University Libraries, Manchester Central Reference Library, and Sheffield Reference Library, for their help in the production of this book.

INDEX

Page numbers in italics indicate illustrations